To Ni
With

Dick

Critical Guides to French Texts

Critical Guides to French Texts

EDITED BY ROGER LITTLE, WOLFGANG VAN EMDEN, DAVID WILLIAMS

PRÉVOST

Manon Lescaut

R.A. Francis

Lecturer in French
University of Nottingham

Grant & Cutler Ltd
1993

ISBN 0 7293 0360 8

I.S.B.N. 84-599-3331-8

DEPÓSITO LEGAL: V. 2.953-1993

Printed in Spain by
Artes Gráficas Soler, S.A., Valencia
for GRANT & CUTLER LTD
55-57 GREAT MARLBOROUGH STREET, LONDON W1V 2AY

Contents

Introduction

Every age makes its own reinterpretation of great literary works, and the kind of interpretation favoured by the present age is well suited to Prévost. *Manon Lescaut*, and indeed his less well-known novels, appear much stronger and subtler once we cease to view them, as a nineteenth-century realist might, as slices of life with fully-rounded characters, and treat them instead as artefacts in which viewpoint is cunningly manipulated to create their own world whose relationship with commonly held notions of reality may be problematic. The problems of interpreting *Manon Lescaut* have always been recognized; as one of the oldest and most enigmatic of the more widely read French novels, it has attracted a critical literature whose range and variety have few parallels. Should the two lovers, Des Grieux and Manon, be treated with the indulgence that Des Grieux as narrator seeks to inspire for them, or are they merely criminals? Does Prévost seriously intend the work to be read as a moral tale, or is it merely a titillating entertainment? And why has *Manon Lescaut* retained its popularity while the rest of Prévost's works have declined into relative obscurity? These and other questions have been asked for years, and there are no agreed answers.

The best way to begin a study of *Manon Lescaut* is by a close examination of how the story is told. It is, of course, a first-person narration, and Prévost's great success in this novel is to have created an interesting situation in which the narrator can tell his story alongside an appropriate manner in which to do it. Both the situation and the manner, however, imply that certain distortions are taking place in the material being presented to us, and we need to consider what kind of distortion might be expected before we can form any judgment of the work's content. I shall therefore begin with a study of the narrator, of the highly elaborate framework in which he is presented, of the narratorial strategy that appears to condition his treatment of the material, and of the ways in which the author behind the narrator may be signalling that we should not be taking the narrator completely on his own estimation. I shall then examine the subject-matter of Des Grieux's narration, to consider how it is likely to have been deformed by the process of narration; the character of Manon herself will be the most important part of this analysis. Next, I shall turn to some of the ideological issues which the work appears to raise, and finally I shall attempt to answer the question of why it has survived so much better than the rest of Prévost's fiction.

Manon Lescaut was first published in 1731, but most modern editions reproduce Prévost's own revised version of 1753, which makes significant changes to the text and adds a whole new episode, that of the Italian prince at the beginning of Part II. The Garnier-Flammarion edition (1992 printing), which I am using for page references because it is probably the most widely used among students today, is no exception to the rule, but the serious student should be aware that the text makes a significantly different impact in its earliest form, and should have access to an edition in which the variants are listed. Other references, in the form (2, p.15), are to the numbered items in the Select Bibliography at the end of this volume.

1. The Framework

Manon Lescaut is the seventh and final volume of a larger novel, the *Mémoires d'un homme de qualité*. This, Prévost's first characteristic work, is a vivid but sometimes rambling piece of fiction, in which a large number of interpolated tales are held together by the adventures of Renoncour, the *homme de qualité* himself, who is the 'I' in the framework narration which opens *Manon Lescaut*. Little is known for certain of the circumstances of composition, but it seems likely that the inclusion of *Manon Lescaut* in the *Mémoires* was an afterthought, determined by commercial reasons. The two moments of contact between Renoncour and Des Grieux do not fit well into the central plot, Renoncour is made to admit that Des Grieux's story has no 'rapport nécessaire' with his own (p.21), and the work's publishing history has amply demonstrated that *Manon Lescaut* can stand alone without the *Mémoires*. Yet criticism would be much impoverished if it denied all serious consideration to the things writers do for commercial reasons. *Manon Lescaut* influences the impact of the *Mémoires*, the framework influences the impact of *Manon Lescaut*, and it is important to see how.

The framework narration follows a pattern often used in the *Mémoires* to integrate an interpolation. Renoncour glimpses Des Grieux twice in contrasting circumstances, first in Pacy on the way to America with Manon, then in Calais on the way back without her, and Des Grieux tells his tale to explain the enigma thus generated. As well as providing a lively and intriguing opening to the story, this framework also establishes a certain relationship between Renoncour and Des Grieux, one which influences the way the story is told. To understand this situation, it would be helpful to look a little more closely than most modern readers do at the role of Renoncour as established in the rest of the *Mémoires*.

Like Des Grieux, Renoncour has suffered, loved and lost; reduced to an exile and a social outcast owing to his father's *mésalliance*, he has seen his young Turkish bride, Selima, die in an epidemic and has been brought close to suicide by her loss. When he first meets Des Grieux in Pacy he is about fifty years old and in the early stages of retirement in a monastery, undertaken partly for religious reasons, partly as an act of loyalty to Selima and partly as a way of opting out of a harsh world with which he has lost the will to cope. He looks upon his passionate past as a sign of having been specially chosen by Providence (2, p.15), which leads him to a sense that he and other men with similar emotional sensitivity constitute an élite fraternity of soulmates. When two such men meet, they can recognize each other instantly, even before exchanging words, and this is what appears to happen between him and Des Grieux: 'on distingue, au premier coup d'œil, un homme qui a de la naissance et de l'éducation ... Je découvris dans ses yeux, dans sa figure et dans tous ses mouvements, un air si fin et si noble que je me sentis porté naturellement à lui vouloir du bien' (p.27). His first meeting with Rosambert, the bosom friend of his youth, is based on a similar instant sympathy (2, p.29), and it is not without significance that this style of perception extends to Manon, for whom he is tempted to feel 'respect' and 'pitié' (p.26) even as she sits chained among a group of prostitutes. At this stage he can do no more than make himself Des Grieux's accomplice by helping him with money, but the act is in character, for his own family history has convinced him that indulgence is the best policy that fathers can adopt in dealing with passionate young men.

When they meet again in Calais, Renoncour's situation has changed almost as much as Des Grieux's. He has been induced out of retirement to be the tutor of Rosemont, a passionate young marquis, and he is struggling to control his ward's passion for his own Turkish niece, Nadine, which he knows will not be approved by Rosemont's father, an indulgent but cynical aristocrat who closely resembles the father of Des Grieux. Renoncour will in the end succeed in separating Rosemont and Nadine, but at the cost of sacrificing his policy of indulgence, and not without some distastefully equivocal behaviour. Renoncour has thus changed from compliant ally of passionate youth to a stern tutor figure. How this situation affects his reaction to Des Grieux's barely penitent tale of excess the text does not reveal; it ends with Des Grieux's final words, with no attempt to show Renoncour reacting to them. He is not even given the chance to comment on the obvious analogies between Des Grieux's love and that of Rosemont, who has also been present to hear the tale. This is surprising given that elsewhere in the *Mémoires* he does draw the moral lessons of interpolated tales for his ward's benefit. We are, however, offered Renoncour's final reaction in a prefatory text standing outside the course of the narration, the *Avis de l'auteur*. In this moralizing statement he argues that the tale he has to tell is a terrible example of what not to do. The validity of this text as a statement of Prévost's aims has been much debated, but however one resolves that debate, the *Avis* works admirably as a reflection of Renoncour's preoccupations. Much of it, especially the passage in which he bemoans the difficulty of knowing whether or not it is the appropriate moment to practise the theoretically admirable virtues of 'la douceur et l'humanité' (p.22), is more relevant to his own problems as Rosemont's tutor than it is to the case of Des Grieux. It points to the ambivalence of Renoncour himself, who risks going wrong both by over-indulgence and by excessive severity, and if, as critics such as Mylne and Josephs have pointed out (22, 24), there is a discrepancy between Renoncour's kindness to Des Grieux at Pacy and the sterner judgment on him which he expresses in the *Avis*, it is one which springs from an inconsistency at the core of Renoncour's character.

As a result, the reader is presented, before Des Grieux begins his tale, with two contrasting visions of him, the *Avis*'s condemnation of him as 'un jeune aveugle, qui refuse d'être heureux, pour se précipiter volontairement dans les dernières infortunes' (p.21), and Renoncour's vision of him at Pacy as the pale and interesting victim of a passion for a girl who may, despite appearances to the contrary, be a worthy object of passion. This immediately builds an ambivalence into the reader's reaction to Des Grieux which his

subsequent narration merely highlights. It also heightens the reader
of the *Mémoires*'s awareness of what is problematic in Renoncour.
The central narrator's own story ends with his return to his monastery once he has completed the separation of Rosemont and Nadine,
to enjoy a calm which one may feel he does not deserve. To end the
novel as a whole by confronting the reader, out of its chronological
context, with this new tale of passion told by a youth who refuses to
be controlled and who, moreover, pushes Renoncour's indulgence
towards passion to unacceptable extremes, is to enhance the reader's
suspicion that Renoncour's final calm is based on an inauthentic
complacency. In this way, *Manon Lescaut* has a significant
subversive effect on the overall impact of the *Mémoires*.

This, however, is less important to my present purpose than
what Renoncour has to offer Des Grieux as an audience for his tale.
Des Grieux appears to respond instinctively to Renoncour, just as
Renoncour does to him. In Pacy, the young man at the depths of his
degradation, who, we shall see, has learned to be economical with
the truth, is remarkably willing to admit to this total stranger the
humiliating fact that he is passionately in love with Manon and has
tried to liberate her by violent means (p.27), an admission which
must run the risk of repelling his interlocutor. In Calais, too, it is
Des Grieux who takes the initiative in offering to tell Renoncour his
story as a debt of honour: 'Monsieur, me dit-il, vous en usez si
noblement avec moi, que je me reprocherais, comme une basse
ingratitude, d'avoir quelque chose de réservé pour vous' (p.30).
There seems to be a basis of openness in this relationship which, we
shall see, Des Grieux does not achieve elsewhere. If so, it is no more
than what one would expect of the mutual transparency of noble
souls which Renoncour achieves elsewhere with Rosambert. Even if
this analogy does not hold good, such openness is still not
implausible. Des Grieux's grief at Manon's death has had time to
pass its first intensity, but not to die away altogether, and he is thus
at a stage where it might be helpful to him to express it by talking
about it. Certainly as he first sets foot back in Europe, he needs to
confront his past. In these circumstances he meets a man who
has been marginally and benevolently involved in his past, who

embodies a certain religious and honourable rectitude, but who is less likely to be censorious than Tiberge or his brother, representatives of the church and the family, both of whom he has wronged. Renoncour's admittedly problematic combination of indulgence and strictness corresponds closely to Des Grieux's mood and needs, and with Renoncour rather than any other possible candidate as narratee, the reader is offered at least the possibility of something approaching an open and honest narration. The next chapter will consider why this is no more than a possibility.

2. The Narration

The first-person narrator is notoriously unreliable. By allowing the novelist to explore a series of events through the limited and often biased viewpoint of a single participant, the device engenders an account which might differ significantly from that given by another participant, or by an omniscient narrator standing outside the action described. It is up to the novelist to decide how much to exploit this potential for unreliability, and Prévost, one of the earliest to see the possibilities, exploits them systematically and subtly.

Des Grieux's story reveals him as a skilled deceiver, who learns his skills very early. No sooner has the young man undergone the *coup de foudre* which begins his love for Manon than he finds himself obliged to lose his rhetorical as well as his sexual innocence. Having naïvely told his straight-laced friend Tiberge of his plans to elope with Manon, he encounters sterner opposition than anticipated, to which his sole response is equivocation; he buys time with a promise to introduce Manon to Tiberge the next day, 's'il se peut', carefully omitting to state that it will not be possible as the elopement is planned for that very night (p.35). Des Grieux perfects his wiles with the aid of the command of rhetoric which he has acquired as a model student in Amiens; as soon as he meets Manon he uses his 'éloquence scolastique' to try to seduce her (p.32), and later we find him training for the priesthood, emerging from his 'exercice public' at the Sorbonne 'couvert de gloire et chargé de compliments' (pp.50–51). To this eloquence he adds a handsome face, a plausible manner and a growing lack of scruple which makes him increasingly willing to use his talents for deceptive purposes. On ten subsequent occasions in the novel he tries to win support from other characters by telling them part of his story, either by word of mouth or by letter; four times to Tiberge (pp.62–63, 86, 150, 160), twice to his father (pp.106, 146), twice to his friend

M. de T... (pp.94, 126–27) and once each to the Superior of Saint-Lazare (p.83) and the captain of the ship taking him to America (p.162). On each of these occasions, he is manipulating the truth in some way. Only once can he be shown actually to lie, when he tells the ship's captain that he and Manon are married, but he is expert in revealing only as much of the truth as he needs to project the required image while concealing the rest. Tiberge, whose awareness of events tends to be two or three steps behind Des Grieux's, is a particularly easy victim; Des Grieux becomes adept at gauging just how much Tiberge already knows, and using this knowledge to obtain money from his friend by hiding other circumstances which would make Tiberge less willing to help if he knew of them (pp.105, 150, 160).

Des Grieux also becomes skilled at tailoring his discourse to his audience. With Tiberge, the cleric, he uses theological terms, drawing him into a debate from which the more slow-witted Tiberge emerges thinking of Des Grieux, misleadingly but more sympathetically, as a Jansenist heretic rather than a dissolute young reprobate (p.89). With his father, he tries to argue that his behaviour is consistent with certain types of honour by citing examples of men in high society who have done worse than he (p.146). Above all, he exercises his skills on M. de T..., a complete stranger whom Des Grieux has judged from his age and rank to be of like character to himself, and targeted as a man of influence who might help him free Manon from the Hôpital. He sets out to make a friend of M. de T..., telling him his story as part of the process. M. de T... is impressed by 'cette marque d'ouverture et de candeur', and the result is that 'nous devînmes amis, sans autre raison que la bonté de nos cœurs et une simple disposition qui porte un homme tendre et généreux à aimer un autre homme qui lui ressemble' (p.95). This looks like the same communion of élite souls which draws Renoncour to Des Grieux, but when the reader considers that it is undertaken by Des Grieux for an interested motive, not for love of M. de T..., that he is prepared, if necessary, to dupe M. de T... into thinking that he will be allowed to share Manon's favours, and that the advice M. de T... subsequently gives Des Grieux pushes him further and further into bad behaviour, it comes to look more like a debased parody of noble friendship, whose vocabulary Des Grieux exploits to impart an air of dignity to a process which in itself does not deserve it.

If so, this raises alarming implications for the tale Des Grieux tells to Renoncour, and hence to us. If he can exploit noble friendship once, he can do so again; we have no guarantee that he is not trying to win help from Renoncour by telling him the story he thinks the hearer wants to hear rather than the whole truth. This is why the relationship with Renoncour described in the previous chapter can do no more than offer a possibility of truthful narration, and I shall later attempt to show that the image Des Grieux projects of himself is indeed one calculated to appeal to Renoncour. Yet there are limits to the degree of mendacity we can expect from Des Grieux. His situation now is different from what it was during his earlier misleading accounts of himself; Manon is dead, and since he is returning home he is in no need of material help. His past record suggests that his sins against the truth are more likely to be of omission than commission, and since any narration achieves coherence only at the cost of leaving out as much as, or more than it includes, Des Grieux is likely to depart from the norm more in degree than in kind. Above all, the text gives no hint of an alternative, more truthful series of events. It could very easily have done so, for instance by confronting Renoncour with another participant in the story who might relate events with a different bias, a device which Prévost does use elsewhere in his fiction. Instead, the author prefers to leave the reader with an uneasy sense that the picture Des Grieux has given is not fully reliable, but cannot be pinned down as false in any specific way. It is no part of Prévost's intention to write a Sherlock Holmes detective story, in which a partial account of events is given and then placed in perspective by a fuller and truer account unravelled by the great sleuth.

This is where we see the inappropriateness of the standards of nineteenth-century realism when we read this work; if we look to it for a mimetic account of a 'true' series of events, we shall be disappointed, for the novel gives us no final or convincing statement of where the 'truth' lies. We see rather a series of events filtered through the mind of Des Grieux, a tormented young man who, even if he is trying to tell the truth — and we should not exclude the possibility — is in no position to see the whole truth, in no fit state of mind to judge it accurately even if he could see it, and so skilled at deceptive rhetoric that it has become an ingrained habit. Prévost's triumph in this work is the access he has allowed us into this tormented mind, and if we are to read his account properly we should concentrate on appreciating this aspect of his achievement rather than on trying to build an alternative version of the facts of the story. We must, however, treat Des Grieux's judgments with extreme caution, and we have the right to assume that relevant factual information is being withheld from us. We do not have the right to supply this information ourselves; such a process could only be conjecture and invention. What we do have the right to do is to try to define the general direction in which the gaps and the distorted judgments are likely to point, but before we can do so, we must consider more closely Des Grieux's narratorial strategy, to decide what exactly he is trying to achieve as he tells his tale to Renoncour.

Des Grieux, before meeting Manon, is an aristocrat, a model student and a possible candidate for a religious vocation. The impact of Manon does not destroy his sense of honour, morality and religion derived from his upbringing; it merely swamps it with an overwhelming passion which has the force of an 'aliénation', a word which does not occur in *Manon Lescaut* but which Prévost uses elsewhere in the sense, common in the eighteenth-century, of a temporary madness, a foreign personality which overtakes a man and obscures his essential self. This has led him into a variety of disreputable forms of behaviour; for love of a girl whom he knows his social peers will not think worthy of him, he has cheated, fornicated, blasphemed, murdered and driven his father to the grave by defying his authority, while all the time remaining fully conscious of the extent of his transgression. Equally humiliating, he has shown weakness by allowing himself to be led into situations which he would not have chosen for himself by a mistress who in some respects appears a stronger character than he.

Now that Manon is dead, he wishes to return to the fold and live a life consistent with the values of his upbringing. Grace, he claims, has finally come to him. Exactly what form this grace takes is a matter of some hesitation on Prévost's part; in the final version of the text, the relevant passage reads: 'le Ciel ... m'éclaira de ses lumières, qui me firent rappeler des idées dignes de ma naissance et de mon éducation ... Je me livrai entièrement aux inspirations de l'honneur' (p.176), but the original 1731 text is significantly different: 'Le Ciel ... m'éclaira des lumières de sa grâce et m'inspira le dessein de retourner à lui par les voies de la pénitence ... Je me livrai entièrement aux exercices de la piété' (*1*, p.243). This constitutes a marked secularization; in 1731 the fold to which Des Grieux is returning is essentially a religious one, with the hint that he will aim at a retreat analogous to Renoncour's, thus placing his career more firmly in the general ambit of the *Mémoires*, whereas in 1753 Des Grieux's concerns appear more secular, a desire for reintegration in his family and class.

Why Prévost made this change is not clear. It could be a response to a more secular public opinion, or an attempt to emancipate *Manon Lescaut* from the context of the *Mémoires*. Most probably, however, it springs from an effort to bring the passage more into line with Des Grieux's character as established by the rest of the narration. If so, the change would certainly be appropriate, for throughout his story Des Grieux appears more upset by his sins against his class than his sins against religion. He makes no sustained attempt to convince his audience of the authenticity of his initial religious vocation. His early promise, he suggests, springs merely from a love of study and a certain 'aversion naturelle pour le vice' (p.30), and he has flirted with Saint-Sulpice only because he has been '[flatté] adroitement' by Tiberge (p.48). Throughout his story, his reactions show much more of the hot-blooded aristocrat conscious of his honour than of the genuine man of religion, and he appears to accept the image. This can be seen in a significant little debate he has with himself about the acceptability of borrowing money:

> Il n'y a qu'une âme lâche qui en soit capable, par une
> bassesse qui l'empêche d'en sentir l'indignité, ou un
> chrétien humble, par un excès de générosité qui le rend
> supérieur à cette honte. Je n'étais ni un homme lâche, ni
> un bon chrétien; j'aurais donné la moitié de mon sang
> pour éviter cette humiliation. (p.103)

The alibi offered by an image of unworldly Christian humility attracts him not at all; it is the shame and dishonour of the process which really upsets him, the sense that in begging for a loan he will be falling short of the standards of his class. By this stage, at the middle of the course of his adventures, little sense of religious motivation is left to him beyond a few nagging background worries and his rhetorical skill. The central conflict facing him is the one between his class values and his love.

The continuation of the debate over borrowing money shows how the problem is resolved:

> Oui, mon sang tout entier ..., je le donnerais plus
> volontiers, sans doute, que de me réduire à de basses
> supplications. Mais il s'agit bien ici de mon sang! Il
> s'agit de la vie et de l'entretien de Manon, il s'agit de
> son amour et de sa fidélité. Qu'ai-je à mettre en balance
> avec elle? Je n'y ai rien mis jusqu'à présent. Elle me
> tient lieu de gloire, de bonheur et de fortune. (p.104)

As regularly happens in his debates with himself, he sees all the objections to pursuing a dishonourable course and then overrules them for the sake of Manon. His rhetoric is put to the service of his love, so that he may transform the inglorious preoccupations of the moment — he needs the money to re-equip himself and his mistress after their escape from prison — into a grand idealistic quest in which mundane present needs are veiled in vague general terms such as 'amour' and 'fidélité', and some higher value appears to be at stake than the shedding of blood in a noble cause which is at the heart of the aristocrat's value-system. This debate is carried out by Des Grieux the protagonist at the time of his adventures, rather than by Des Grieux the narrator — always an important distinction to make, since the difference may have a considerable bearing on the status of his words — but it takes us to the central problem of his narratorial strategy. As he returns to Europe, forced to take stock of his situation, to come to terms with his past behaviour and to work out a way of living again within his class, he must do one of two things. Either he must repent of his past, and accept that he has betrayed his noble values by pursuing an unworthy objective, or he must find some way of suggesting that all the admittedly wrong things he has done were done in the name of some other code of values through which he can reclaim some of his lost dignity. It is clear that he has opted for the second alternative. Though he admits his misdeeds, he cannot bring himself to much display of remorse or penitence; the relative infrequence in his discourse of these notions, with their strong religious connotations, is further evidence that Prévost was right in 1753 to play down the religious aspect of his return. Instead, he uses his considerable verbal felicity to build an image of himself as a man of superior sensitivity who ultimately achieves his own idiosyncratic form of heroism. He may have forfeited his claim to acceptance within the nobility, the élite which society recognizes as superior, but he is bidding for a place in Renoncour's élite of men of feeling, one which will always be likely to overlap with the nobility, but which cannot be fully identified with it.

Des Grieux is keen to project an image of himself as a developing character. At the time of his *coup de foudre*, he reminds us, he is a child, with little experience and immature responses. 'Je vois bien que je ne suis qu'un enfant', he declares to his father after being confronted with Manon's first betrayal of him (p.46); such an innocent as he can hardly be blamed for being led astray in a wicked world, he seems to imply. As his adventures proceed, however, he loses this innocence. 'Un peu d'expérience' helps him when he next sets up house with Manon (p.55), and 'l'âge et l'expérience' enable him to confront his father boldly from his prison in the Châtelet (p.143). Alongside his growing practical competence, he would have us believe that the character of his love is also growing in maturity. At the outset, the facts of his story barely allow him to avoid giving the impression of a weak, easily led youth whose infatuation makes him the prey of a flighty lass, at best irresponsible and at worst depraved, for whose possession he will sink to any depths. Yet even in surrendering to her whims he can hint that he is demonstrating his superiority. 'Où trouver un barbare qu'un repentir si vif et si tendre n'eût pas touché?' he exclaims when recalling how she returned to him in Saint-Sulpice (p.54); to fail to respond to the qualities of love and emotion which she appears to be offering him would relegate him to a lower order of humanity. Similarly, what some might see as his obsessive desire to possess his beloved is transformed through his words into a noble and meritorious constancy: 'Je me trouve le plus malheureux de tous les hommes, par cette même constance dont je devais attendre le plus doux de tous les sorts, et les plus parfaites récompenses de l'amour' (p.36). Most significantly of all, he is at pains to underline what he is sacrificing for her sake:

> Je vais perdre ma fortune et ma réputation pour toi, je le prévois bien; je lis ma destinée dans tes beaux yeux; mais de quelles pertes ne serai-je pas consolé par ton amour! Les faveurs de la fortune ne me touchent point; la gloire me paraît une fumée; tous mes projets de vie ecclésiastique étaient de folles imaginations; enfin tous les biens différents de ceux que j'espère avec toi sont des biens méprisables, puisqu'ils ne sauraient tenir un moment, dans mon cœur, contre un seul de tes regards.
>
> (pp.52–53)

This eloquent tirade shows Des Grieux with the full awareness of a tragic hero accepting his fate, agreeing to sacrifice this world, and possibly the next world into the bargain, for the sake of a love which

engenders superior values of its own. His great theological debate
with Tiberge in Saint-Lazare (p.86 ff.) works in the same direction,
showing him weighing up heavenly bliss against worldly bliss with
Manon and consciously opting for the latter.

None of this is enough to absolve him from the charge of irresponsible licentiousness, of preferring a transitory, and presumably
basely physical satisfaction to his eternal salvation. Des Grieux tries
to counter this charge by hinting that his love changes in character,
the turning point being their second arrest and incarceration in the
Châtelet. Until then, all his efforts and ingenuity have been directed
to ensuring his physical possession of Manon and preventing her
from going off with rich rivals, but in face of this crisis, whose
seriousness he fully recognizes, the emphasis switches from
possession to protection. 'Ce n'est pas moi qui suis à plaindre', he
says to her as they are separated. 'Quelques mois de prison ne
m'effraient nullement ... Mais c'est pour toi, ma chère âme, que
mon cœur s'intéresse' (p.142). Whether or not this change of
emphasis makes any difference to the way he actually behaves is a
moot point, but it does help him to impart a veneer of respectability
to the series of actions he is about to undertake, which in the eyes of
his social peers are the most compromising of all: his rupture with
his father, his attempt to free Manon by violence and his decision to
accompany her to America. The last of these, yet again, is presented
with the full panoply of a tragic hero, in the declaration of intent
which he makes, rather incongruously, to the hired thug who was to
have helped him to liberate Manon:

> Tout le monde me persécute ou me trahit ... Je n'ai plus
> de fond à faire sur personne. Mes malheurs sont au
> comble; il ne me reste plus que de m'y soumettre. Ainsi,
> je ferme les yeux à toute espérance. Puisse le Ciel
> récompenser votre générosité! Adieu, je vais aider mon
> mauvais sort à consommer ma ruine, en y courant moi-
> même volontairement. (p.157)

The new element in this tirade is its last word, 'volontairement'. Previously, Des Grieux has been content to suggest that his bad behaviour has not been committed with the full assent of his will; either Manon's whims or some hostile fate have taken the brunt of the blame. Now, he is taking charge of his destiny with full lucidity, and the essence of his bid for heroic stature lies in his transformation of extreme worldly degradation into the pursuit of a love which, as it moves towards its tragic dénouement, becomes more and more idealized. Manon's love, too, appears to have acquired a new maturity on the road to the port of embarkation — I shall have more to say on this in a later chapter — and their life together in America becomes an idyll of mutual selfless love between two irreproachable colonists whose sole desire is to be married and lead a blameless life in atonement for their past. Manon's last night alive, when they vie with each other under the stars to tend each other's needs (p.173), offers a moving picture of harmony we have never seen them achieve before and the ultimate validation of the quality of their love. Small wonder, then, that even in his decision to return to his family, 'je renonce volontairement à [mener une vie] jamais plus heureuse' (p.174). Manon's love, for him, represents a supreme value, and his will henceforth will be directed at preserving its integrity by abstaining from any other happiness, just as Renoncour, in his retreat, fosters his memories of Selima. Thus it is that Des Grieux seeks to transform himself into a hero of love; it is a vision of himself that he can live with, and it also tells Renoncour what he is likely to want to hear.

Such, at least, is the image Des Grieux seeks to project. How far it is acceptable I shall consider in the next chapter, but before approaching that question, a few other considerations should be raised. First, Des Grieux's image of himself implies a corresponding and equally controversial image of Manon. I have deliberately said little of her so far, but her character obviously raises major issues which will have to be explored later. Secondly, it is worth reflecting further on Des Grieux's manner of self-presentation. It is not clear whether we are meant to conclude that the image he projects to Renoncour is fully formed in advance, or improvised as he tells his

tale to this sympathetic but unexpected listener. Jaccard makes a
strong case in favour of the latter (*21*), and there is certainly a
spontaneity in his narration, a suggestion that he is still in the
process of thinking through problems which he has never yet had a
chance to voice. At the same time, his past amply demonstrates his
skill at arranging his thoughts in words and projecting a calculated
image. Old habits die hard, and it would not be implausible for
many of his thoughts to be prearranged in his mind, carried over, as
it were, from his earlier deceptive accounts of himself. As a result,
the tone of his narrative wavers between the naïve and the knowing,
in a disturbing way which tends to evoke a complex and uncertain
response in the reader.

It is, however, the tension between these opposing tones which
engenders the highly individual combination of lyrical and analytic
style which is an important part of the work's appeal. Des Grieux's
state of mind as he narrates is still dominated by intense emotions
which have lost little of their poignant urgency, but he has had some
time to reflect on his situation and arrange his thoughts. His
narration is supposed to be spoken, not written, which does not
mean that he is allowed hesitations and colloquialisms which might
undermine his aristocratic image, but it does allow a certain
directness in the expression of emotion which in the written word
might become veiled. The intensity of his feelings at times goes
beyond his verbal ability to express them, most memorably at the
moment of Manon's death, the ultimate disaster, which he is too
choked by emotion to be able to record:

> N'exigez point de moi que je vous décrive mes senti-
> ments, ni que je vous rapporte ses dernières expressions.
> Je la perdis; je reçus d'elle des marques d'amour, au
> moment même qu'elle expirait. C'est tout ce que j'ai la
> force de vous apprendre de ce fatal et déplorable
> événement. (p.174)

On the other hand, the polished and controlled diction of these
sentences suggests that he is far from incoherent. This highly

articulate young man has had every motivation and every oppor-
tunity to think about himself and order his reflections. He neither
attempts nor achieves the detached retrospective lucidity of that
other great contemporary unreliable first-person narrator, Marivaux's Marianne, who is presented as standing at many years'
distance from the events she describes, with ample time to build a
reflective, though not unbiased image. Nor does his style reflect the
spontaneity of a first reaction such as one might find in the letters of
a Clarissa or a Saint-Preux, writing under the immediate impact of
events. The delicate balance he strikes between these two extremes
can be seen in the narratorial reflection on his mood following his
discovery of Manon's letter telling him that she has left him for G...
M...:

> Je demeurai, après cette lecture, dans un état qui me
> serait difficile à décrire car j'ignore encore aujourd'hui
> par quelle espèce de sentiments je fus alors agité. Ce fut
> une de ces situations uniques auxquelles on n'a rien
> éprouvé qui soit semblable. On ne saurait les expliquer
> aux autres, parce qu'ils n'en ont pas l'idée; et l'on a
> peine à se les bien démêler à soi-même, parce qu'étant
> seules de leur espèce, cela ne se lie à rien dans la
> mémoire, et ne peut même être rapproché d'aucun sen-
> timent connu. Cependant, de quelque nature que fussent
> les miens, il est certain qu'il devait y entrer de la
> douleur, du dépit, de la jalousie et de la honte. Heureux
> s'il n'y fût pas entré encore plus d'amour! (p.70)

This passage, paradoxically, gives a remarkably eloquent impression of how words fail him. Despite his disclaimers, he does achieve
an analytic statement of the complex mixture of emotions besetting
him, and he combines it with an admirable lyrical intensity,
expressing both his discomfiture at the time of events as he attempts
to come to terms with this distressing new experience, and also his
perplexity at the time of narration, as he tries to suggest his present
emotion as he recalls events, with the subtle hint that if he can

experience such esoteric and intense feelings, he must be a creature of superior sensitivity. The complexity of response elicited by a passage of this nature gives the measure of Prévost's stylistic achievement in this work. Des Grieux is given a highly specific situation in which to narrate, charged with all kinds of conflicting pressures, and with it exactly the right style in which to reflect these pressures, without ever sinning against the greatest requirement of all, that of expressing himself well. In a supreme gesture of self-confidence, Prévost makes Renoncour declare that Des Grieux related his adventures 'de la meilleure grâce du monde' (p.30). His self-confidence is justified.

3. Judging the Narration

In the face of all this eloquence, the reader has to decide how much of it he will take on trust. We have seen that there is no explicit statement of any version of the facts counter to Des Grieux's, and the question at once arises as to whether any counter-interpretation can be authoritative. To put it another way, does Prévost, as author, seek to project a vision of events distinct from Des Grieux's? It is notoriously difficult to determine authorial intention, especially with an author like Prévost who appears to have cultivated a deliberate elusiveness, nor is it necessarily helpful, when it can be determined, to use intention as a guide to how the reader should react. It is more misleading still, however, to assume that the principal voice, in this or indeed any other fictional work, is a straightforward mouthpiece for the author, and Prévost's art appears much more impressive to the reader who succeeds in separating the author's vision from Des Grieux's. This is not an area for clear-cut definition, but it is possible to consider ways in which such a vision might be projected, and that is what I shall attempt to do in this chapter.

The simplest device the author can use is giving the narrator the rope with which to hang himself, by allowing Des Grieux to develop his arguments to the fullest extent and thus permit the reader to judge exactly how flawed they are. This appears to be happening with some of Des Grieux's self-justifications, which reveal themselves to be so outrageous that it is hard to imagine them being taken seriously. An example might be the excuse he gives for living on his wits prior to his career as a card-sharper, which he claims is merely taking advantage of the fact that the rich are made fools by Providence in order to give a chance to the clever poor to redress the balance by exploiting them (p.59). A little later, he manages to avoid giving a justification for his swindling of G... M..., on the grounds that it is a lesser misdeed than his card-sharping which he has already justified by the argument summarized above:

> Quoiqu'à mes propres yeux cette action fût une véritable
> friponnerie, ce n'était pas la plus injuste que je crusse
> avoir à me reprocher. J'avais plus de scrupule sur
> l'argent que j'avais acquis au jeu. Cependant nous
> profitâmes aussi peu de l'un que de l'autre, et le Ciel
> permit que la plus légère de ces deux injustices fût la
> plus rigoureusement punie. (p.77)

Not only does this neat piece of casuistry distract attention from the immediate issue, it also hints cheekily at a flaw in the operation of divine justice. Excessive cleverness of this type always risks being counterproductive, and it is hardly likely that a *bien-pensant* audience in Prévost's day would be impressed by the proto-socialism and near blasphemy of these arguments. Though one cannot say with certainty that readers were meant to react critically to them, Prévost must have known that there was a strong possibility that they would. Another, more succinct example is Des Grieux's bland refusal to shoulder any of the blame for killing the porter whom he guns down during his escape from Saint-Lazare; he loftily blames the Superior for calling the porter to his aid — 'Voilà de quoi vous êtes cause, mon Père' — and tells Lescaut that it is his fault for bringing him a loaded pistol (p.92). Here, his argument has some validity; he had indeed asked for an unloaded pistol, and it is probably true to say that eighteenth-century novel readers would be less shocked than those of our own age by the murder of a *comparse* from the lower orders. Yet the sheer incongruity between the nature of the deed and its perpetrator's almost childish lack of any sense of responsibility or remorse still has a capacity to shock and to inspire doubts. Significantly, all the examples quoted in this paragraph are reflections made by Des Grieux at the time of his adventures, rather than subsequently as narrator. This means that he has the chance to distance himself from them, with the benefit of hindsight. He does not choose to take this chance, preferring to leave his dubious arguments to make what impact they can without drawing too much attention to their weaknesses, but at least, by refraining from throwing his full narratorial weight behind them, he is leaving open the possibility of dissociating himself from them.

Another way of subverting the narrator's image of himself lies in the choice of incidents for inclusion in the story, a choice which is nominally Des Grieux's but is, of course, really the responsibility of the author. Des Grieux's basic strategy, that of presenting himself with the dignity of a hero, requires linguistic manipulation. He must speak of himself in the stylistic registers associated with traditional heroism, in genres such as tragedy and the heroic novel of the seventeenth century. Yet he has to live in a sordid everyday world which the heroic genres do not have the language to describe, which means that he frequently has to veil the baser aspects of his story in circumlocutions, euphemisms and other types of veiled allusion. This is a process which can occasionally be seen at work in discrepancies between the 1731 and 1753 versions, for Prévost's revision moves in the general direction of greater refinement and a few new euphemisms are introduced. In 1731, for instance, when G... M... wishes to complete his conquest of Manon, 'il proposa à Manon d'aller au lit' (*1*, p.224); in 1753, this is reduced to: 'il parla d'amour et d'impatience' (p.77). A similar avoidance of a crude reality by veiled terminology occurs when Des Grieux, newly arrived at Saint-Lazare, haughtily declares to the Superior: 'Mon Père, ... point d'indignités. Je perdrai mille vies avant que d'en souffrir une' (p.78). An audience of the 1730s would not need to be told that this is an attempt to forestall the humiliating prospect of being flogged. Nevertheless the very fact that the allusion is there at all — and it could easily have been omitted — reminds the reader that the proud young man is in fact in a most undignified situation.

Other details, equally superfluous to the development of the plot, seem to have been included for the sole purpose of projecting a less heroic image of Des Grieux than the one which his discourse suggests, for instance his inability to resist arrest at the hands of G... M... because he is in bed with Manon and his sword is entangled in his belt (p.138), or his jeopardizing of the plan to rescue Manon from the Hôpital by forgetting to bring a spare pair of breeches for her male attire, which obliges him to walk out of prison without his own, preserving decency beneath a long overcoat (p.99). Perhaps the starkest contrast between appearance and reality occurs when the escape from the Hôpital is completed. The driver of the cab Des Grieux has hired asks where to take them, whereupon Des Grieux permits himself a rhetorical flourish: 'Touche au bout du monde, ... et mène-moi quelque part où je ne puisse jamais être séparé de Manon' (p.99). All this does is awaken the cab-driver's suspicions and spark off a dispute about the fare; Des Grieux's *style noble* merely draws attention to the discrepancy between the realities of his situation and the way he would like to see himself. With details such as this punctuating his account, it is hard for him to sustain the desired heroic image.

The above illustration shows the use which can be made of dialogue. Prévost is much less interested than contemporaries such as Marivaux in highlighting differences of speech patterns, and in general Des Grieux makes sparing use of direct speech. Many of the conversations he reproduces take the form of reported speech, with occasional moves into direct speech for the sake of variety or in order to highlight an important moment. Normally, Des Grieux uses this technique in the interests of his own strategy; the more disturbing aspects of Manon's character are muted because so many of her words are withheld from the reader, and in the debate with Tiberge in Saint-Lazare Des Grieux gives himself an unfair advantage by quoting his own words in direct speech and those of Tiberge in reported speech. Just occasionally, however, other characters are allowed to speak in their own words and in a way which suggests an alternative vision. After introducing Manon to G... M..., Lescaut deflates Des Grieux's indignant challenge with a simple 'Là! que vous êtes vif!' (p.71). More elaborately, his father mocks his prowess as a lover by his detailed calculation of how many, or rather how few days Manon had been faithful to him before betraying him to B... (p.43). Such passages are rarely extensive, but they are enough to remind the reader that Des Grieux's story told from another viewpoint might look very different.

The most important means at the author's disposal to modify our perception of Des Grieux is his ability to manipulate the overall structuring of the story. It is increasingly appreciated by critics, notably Betts and Singerman (*5, 33*), that Prévost's novels are held together by a complex network of parallel incidents and characters whose resemblances and subtle differences throw a light on each other which it is the reader's responsibility to interpret for himself. We have already seen one example of this in the way that Des Grieux's relationship with M. de T... casts doubts on the authenticity of the noble transparency apparently established between Des Grieux and Renoncour, but the most obvious example is the way the whole novel's structure hinges on a certain type of repeated episode. Five times in the novel, Des Grieux has to contend with a richer or more powerful rival for the possession of Manon, each time with a slightly different outcome, a comparison of the different episodes sheds light on the evolution in the characters that is taking place, and the resultant image is not necessarily the one which Des Grieux would have chosen. The repetitiousness of the plot in itself signals the obsessive incorrigibility of the lovers' behaviour, and Des Grieux's changing reaction to his rivals — total innocence in face of B..., reluctant connivance in the swindling of G... M... and active involvement in the swindling of young G... M... — suggests a pattern of degeneration which runs directly contrary to the picture of heroic development which the narrator tries to suggest. Some readers become irritated with the repetitious nature of the plot of this novel, but there seems little doubt that Prévost is using it as a conscious structuring principle. The process is especially clear with the extra episode included in the 1753 edition, that of the Italian prince who becomes the third of Manon's suitors, separating the attempts of the two G... M...s. It was inserted, Prévost tells us, 'pour la plénitude d'un des principaux caractères' (p.23), and the impact it has on our perception of Manon is an issue which I shall shortly have to face. My present point is that this late addition, made at a stage in Prévost's career when his technique was more fully formed than in 1731, is made to reflect other episodes particularly closely, especially Manon's involvement with B... The scene between the

lovers as Manon awaits the arrival of the Italian prince (pp.113 ff.)
has strong parallels with the supper scene which Manon knows will
be interrupted by representatives of Des Grieux's family who have
been alerted by B... (pp.39 ff.), with the important difference that
one episode shows Manon's fickleness and the other her fidelity. We
shall see that the Italian prince episode also throws a disturbing
light on Manon's involvement with young G... M....

Those who read *Manon Lescaut* in the context of the
Mémoires will discover that the network of parallels extends further.
The two most substantial of the other interpolated tales, those of
Rosambert and Dom Manuel of Portugal, are also centred on
passionate young men whose dissolute behaviour brings them into
conflict with the value-systems of their society; Manuel in particular
has something of Des Grieux's refusal to accept responsibility for
disasters of which he may well be considered the cause. It is not
unusual in episodic novels of this type for the interpolated tales to
offer tragic variations on themes established by the central
narration, whose hero, of course, has to have the flexibility to
survive a whole series of adventures, and *Manon Lescaut* is a good
example of the type. Des Grieux also parallels Rosemont as a high-
born young man driven into criminality by his love for an unsuitable
girl. It is the parallels with Renoncour himself, however, which are
most telling. Renoncour is, we have seen, a man of passion, though
now chastened in his old age, and some of his views on the subject
of passion are close to Des Grieux's. The difference is that Des
Grieux carries them to extremes. Both believe that passion is
inspired by some supernatural force, be it Providence or fatality, but
Renoncour thinks it is subject to rational control; Des Grieux does
not. Renoncour cautiously asserts that 'l'amour ne nous rend point
criminels, lorsque l'objet est légitime' (2, p.15), but Des Grieux
throws caution to the winds and claims that 'l'amour est une
passion innocente' (p.72). Renoncour believes in an élite of sensi-
tive souls, but he never develops the idea as forcefully or explicitly
as Des Grieux does in the famous passage evoking his arrival at
Saint-Lazare, where intense shame makes him reflect on the greater
range of emotions experienced by 'les personnes d'un caractère plus

noble' (p.79). Des Grieux, as I have hinted, may make Renoncour look a crabbed old compromiser who does not deserve his calm, but that does not stop Renoncour from making Des Grieux look a dangerous fanatic who has strayed too far from the *juste milieu*. Prévost does not attempt to decide between the two; he is content to let each subvert the other and leave the reader to decide.

Now that we have seen something of the techniques whereby Des Grieux's image of himself may be undermined, it is possible to draw some conclusions about the kind of case which could be made against him. Three lines of argument seem possible. The first is that his egocentric passion and the rhetorical facility which enables him to substitute words for realities have blinded him to the true nature of his situation and to the extent of his responsibility for events. This charge is best developed by attempting to view the story from a perspective other than that of Des Grieux himself, especially that of Manon; I shall attempt to show where this may lead in the next chapter. Secondly, it is possible to reduce much of Des Grieux's self-justification to an assumption that his status as a lover reveals the greatness of his soul and thus cleanses him of the stains which deeds such as his might leave on a lesser man. An action with bad results can be excused if it is carried out for a good end such as love, and both he and Manon, he implies, are something more than the sum total of their actions. This is an assumption which an eighteenth-century readership would be more likely to find convincing than the average reader of today. Many of Prévost's narrators use it, including Renoncour himself in the conclusion to the *Avis de l'auteur*, where he argues that his good moral intentions in telling this story are sufficient justification even if its results are less edifying than he hopes: 'si la réflexion que je viens de faire est solide, elle me justifie; si elle est fausse, mon erreur sera mon excuse' (p.23). Such arguments are based on a vision of the human personality which Deloffre and Picard have termed essentialism (*1*, p.cx), the notion that, whatever a man's actions may amount to, there is at some deep level within him a basic selfhood which remains unmodified by them. The term is best understood as an opposite to Sartre's concept of existentialism, whereby personality is

wholly constituted by the sum total of a man's actions, and to a
generation reared on existentialism, Des Grieux can appear little
other than a textbook case of what Sartre would have called
mauvaise foi. Several recent critical interpretations, notably those of
Monty and Creignou (*23, 8*), present him in this light, insisting that
he should be judged by actions for which he cannot simply shift the
blame to other people or an outside fatality.

A third line of attack, probably the most interesting to be
developed by recent critics, is to undermine Des Grieux's image of
himself as a hero of love by casting doubt on the quality of his love.
According to this view, the battle in Des Grieux between the values
of his class and his love is less decisively resolved in favour of the
latter than at first sight appears. He retains a strong desire to regain
acceptability within his class, doing all he can to keep the lines of
communication open until the last possible moment, but after his
decision to accompany Manon to America makes this no longer
possible, his only hope of salvaging any form of dignity at all is to
develop a heroic image of his love which will at least have more
chance of appealing to his aristocratic peers than the image of a
dissolute rebel. To achieve this, he must of course carry his love to
its fullest extent and maintain his constancy to Manon through the
depths of degradation. If, however, his main requirement has
become the ability to make his love look heroic, he has less need
than before of the person of Manon. His vision of Manon, we shall
see, has been evolving, and in the direction of idealization; his ideal
love needs an ideal object, and Manon as a real woman could be
something of an inconvenience. It is also possible to argue that by
the time they leave for America, he has come to hate her for her
frequent infidelities. It therefore suits his ends that she should die in
America, and it may even be that, once there, he engineers the
situation so that she does die, but in circumstances allowing him to
complete the idealization both of her image and of his own, so that
he can return to France with a view of himself that he can project
with some confidence to his peers, and at the same time live with
himself. Elements of this case are argued by Donohoe, Jaccard and
Segal (*10, 21, 27*), and it represents the most insidious charge yet to

be laid against Des Grieux, casting doubt on the love which he has tried to suggest is his very essence.

Whether the case is entirely convincing is another matter. It is persuasive, it raises issues which are difficult to refute and it risks making many other readings look naïve, yet if it successfully defines what Des Grieux wants to achieve, one is forced to conclude that he has chosen a most roundabout way of achieving it, and it runs so radically counter to the overt thrust of Des Grieux's self-portrayal that one cannot help feeling that if Prévost had really wanted the reader to come to such a conclusion, he would have found more explicit ways of signalling it. It seems likely that, for all his signalled criticisms, Prévost retained a considerable degree of sympathy for Des Grieux and would not wish to deny all quality to his love. Yet what Prévost intended is not the decisive factor. Each age interprets great works according to its own lights, and if the characters Prévost created have a sufficient measure of human truth, it will be possible to interpret them coherently according to the conceptual codes of another age, be it Sartrian philosophy or the psychoanalytic approach brilliantly applied by Segal, which attributes subconscious motives to Des Grieux in ways which would have been completely foreign to Prévost's thought processes. If such approaches appear to harmonize well with the data given by the text and to help us to read it in a fresh light even when they go far beyond anything which is at all likely to have been Prévost's conscious intention, it tells us something about the richness, the complexity and above all the ambiguity of the character that Prévost has created. No single interpretation can do justice to Des Grieux. He remains as Renoncour says, 'un mélange de vertus et de vices' (p.22), whose linguistic skill at the same time hides much and reveals much; more, sometimes, perhaps, than he wants to reveal.

4. A Distorted Vision

If the picture Des Grieux gives of himself cannot be trusted, his picture of the world in which he moves is equally suspect. Quite apart from his willingness to manipulate his material in his own interests, he is simply not the kind of character one would expect to devote attention to the world outside himself. Wrapped up as he is in his own concerns, with little care for anything unrelated to his immediate problems, he will not be likely to have much attention to spare for inessentials. This is an area in which eighteenth-century first-person narration differs radically from the nineteenth-century model of fiction in which an omniscient narrator with no role to play as a character in the story can indulge in detailed observation and social documentation. In *Manon Lescaut*, the character of the narrator combines with a classical distaste for physical portrayal to rule out extended descriptions. Yet Des Grieux needs to give some impression of his environment and the people with whom he deals as part of his whole process of image-projection. Here again, without presuming to be able to build a 'truer' version than Des Grieux can provide, we need to consider what kinds of distortion might be at work.

Without ever pushing itself into the foreground, the Paris environment achieves a considerable presence in the novel. As we shall see in the next chapter, it is an important part of Des Grieux's self-justification that he should show himself operating against a backdrop of the seedier areas of Paris life, a life which he does not need to describe in detail because it is recent history and a world familiar to his readers, but whose presence can tactfully be made tangible by the use of real place names, allusions to real institutions such as gambling houses and prisons, and hints — probably misleading — that a scandalously true story is being told by the use of discreet initials rather than names to designate some of the characters. Prévost himself, something of a historian, took pains to project a convincing illusion by being as accurate and consistent in his treatment of time and place as the demands of his fictional situation allowed, and Paris imposes itself upon the reader more effectively in *Manon Lescaut* than in most novels of Prévost's generation.

With other, less familiar environments, Prévost reserved the right to manipulate the facts to serve his own purposes, and this is what happens with the American episodes. Louisiana being a faraway country of which his audience knew very little, Prévost could allow himself, in his few brief descriptive touches, to follow his imagination. His initial evocation of the 'campagnes stériles et inhabitées' which confront the lovers on their arrival (p.163) is probably closer to the truth than the glowing official propaganda statements currently being made about the new colony being established there, but the reason why it is included is not for documentary purposes; it is to give an advance hint that Louisiana will not be the utopia for which the lovers hope. More tellingly, Manon's death takes place in a sandy treeless plain (p.173), which is an appropriately bleak setting for the event, but it does not correspond to the marshy territory which in fact surrounded New Orleans. Whether this is a case of Prévost inventing to fill a gap in his knowledge or deliberately sacrificing facts to expressivity we may never know, but at the same time as he was probably writing *Manon Lescaut* he was working on another novel, *Cleveland*, which includes extensive American scenes which he undoubtedly did research, so it is fully possible that this is a deliberate distortion.

In such cases one should distinguish, perhaps, between distortions introduced by the author for a poetic purpose and those which should be attributed to the narrator for a rhetorical purpose, but when we turn to the presentation of the other characters in the story, we are firmly back with the latter. Des Grieux wishes to talk about himself, not other people, and the images he projects of other people are manifestly inadequate as fully rounded characterizations, transparently subject to the role he needs to make them play in the story. Anyone who helps him is a noble and admirable friend and anyone

who crosses him is an utter villain, thus M. de T..., whose influence
on Des Grieux is probably just as baneful as Lescaut's, is projected
as an ideal companion, whereas old G... M..., admittedly no paragon
but arguably more sinned against than sinning, becomes a 'vieux
tigre' with no redeeming features (p.141). This simplistic process
becomes slightly more complex when dealing with Tiberge and his
father, incarnations of the values of church and class respectively
and thus figures of authority to whom it ill behoves the supposedly
penitent narrator to show disrespect, but at the same time obstacles
to his passion whom he has deceived and flouted. The solution is
not to avoid portraying the quarrels with his father, the tricks played
on Tiberge, but to surround these discreditable acts with palliative
narratorial comment emphasizing the excellence of his adversaries
compared with his own unworthiness, and to highlight those points
of the story where he can be shown in harmony with them. Both of
them, for instance, confront him in prison, Tiberge in Saint-Lazare,
his father in the Châtelet, and on each occasion he engages in a
major self-justifying debate, at the end of which he is at pains to
show that he has made his point and is still on good terms with his
adversary. Scenes of violent rupture never take place without a
touch to soften the blow; if on their last meeting he calls his father a
'père barbare et dénaturé', it is with the distancing qualification that
he said it 'dans mon transport' (p.154), and though Tiberge at one
point walks out indignantly on his incorrigible friend, Des Grieux's
narratorial reflection dwells on the 'retour vers le bien' which, however transitorily, Tiberge's words inspire (p.67). Des Grieux makes
a special point of praising both Tiberge and his father effusively in
his narratorial comments, sometimes to such an extent that one
suspects him of protesting too much. The following remarks on
Tiberge are a case in point:

> Rien n'est plus admirable, et ne fait plus d'honneur à la
> vertu, que la confiance avec laquelle on s'adresse aux
> personnes dont on connaît parfaitement la probité. On
> sent qu'il n'y a point de risque à courir. Si elles ne sont
> pas toujours en état d'offrir du secours, on est sûr qu'on

> en obtiendra du moins de la bonté et de la compassion.
> Le cœur, qui se ferme avec tant de soin au reste des
> hommes, s'ouvre naturellement en leur présence,
> comme une fleur s'épanouit à la lumière du soleil, dont
> elle n'attend qu'une douce influence. (p.61)

This uncharacteristically long narratorial reflection has an unctu-
ousness which smacks of hypocrisy. It is aimed to suggest that Des
Grieux reveals something of his own essential merit by maintaining
an open, transparent relationship with his virtuous friend. Yet when
we recall that he hardly ever approaches Tiberge during his adventures without trying to deceive him or exploit his good nature, and
that he generally succeeds owing to Tiberge's guileless probity, we
may suspect that more than a hint of irony is involved. Des Grieux
is simply not capable of detached and disinterested character
portrayal.

It is essential to bear this in mind in approaching the problem
which more than any other has fascinated readers of this novel over
the ages: what should be made of the character of Manon? It is not
just for reasons of shorthand that a work correctly titled the *Histoire
du Chevalier des Grieux et de Manon Lescaut* has become known
by the name of its heroine; although Prévost's main interest was
almost certainly in the problems of Des Grieux, the enigmatic
charm of Manon has proved a most effective scene-stealer.

The standard novel heroine in the generations preceding
Prévost was a princess pure as driven snow, and Prévost's original-
ity is to have Des Grieux apply language appropriate to such a princess to a girl of much lower birth and dubious moral standards,
leaving the reader to decide how appropriate this language is. Like
many questions I have raised in this study, that of Manon is not one
which permits of a single authoritative answer. We see Manon
almost entirely through the eyes of Des Grieux; the quantity and
enthusiasm of his rivals confirm that she is attractive to men, but
that tells us little, and Renoncour's brief glimpse of her at Pacy, as a
chained prostitute who looks superior to her situation, merely leads
him to reflect inconclusively on the 'caractère incompréhensible des

femmes' (p.29). His vision is merely a reflection of Des Grieux's, with nothing authoritative about it, leaving the reader locked in Des Grieux's defective viewpoint and forced to accept that he can never know the 'real' Manon, if such there be. All the reader can do is analyse the kind of vision of Manon that Des Grieux projects and try to define the processes at work.

Many aspects of Manon are never discussed at all. There is no physical description of her, which is not surprising within the conventions of the eighteenth-century novel, especially if one remembers that Des Grieux is talking to Renoncour who already knows what she looks like. We know nothing of her parents; Prévost seems even to have hesitated over her social class, making her 'point de qualité, quoique d'assez bonne naissance' in 1731 (*1*, p.215), but 'd'une naissance commune' in 1753 (p.33), a demotion which seems fully appropriate in the light of her brother's coarse and unrefined character. More significantly, we are told few of her adventures which do not directly involve Des Grieux. In the account of their first meeting, he does not say what form was taken by 'son penchant au plaisir, qui s'était déjà déclaré' (p.32); at their reunion in the Hôpital, although 'la pauvre Manon me raconta ses aventures, et je lui appris les miennes' (p.97), he shows no interest in passing on the details of what has happened to Manon in prison. His inability or unwillingness to grasp Manon's life away from himself is made perfectly explicit; her decision to seek him out in Saint-Sulpice, he says, can be attributed to 'un reste de curiosité, ou peut-être quelque repentir de m'avoir trahi (je n'ai jamais pu démêler lequel de ces deux sentiments)' (p.50) — this despite the fact that she does explicitly tell him something of what led her to come to Saint-Sulpice (p.53). It is no coincidence that all of these omissions are in areas where the truth is likely to be counter to the noble image of Manon that he wants to leave with his audience or to hold in his own mind. The notion of a complex Manon, with more facets to her personality than those she chooses to present to him, is simply more than he can cope with.

The image he evolves of her is itself complex, however, and it springs from the conflicting needs he must satisfy in the building of it. On the one hand, he needs a scapegoat. He has been drawn into acts he would rather not have committed, and in his quest for factors outside himself on which to pin the blame, he turns to Manon's frivolity and irresponsibility as much as he does to fatality, society, Lescaut, his rivals or whatever other target seems convenient. It is Manon who persuades him to abandon Saint-Sulpice, to connive at the swindling of G... M..., to follow M. de T...'s ill-conceived scheme of spending the night in young G... M...'s bed, all of them disastrous deeds he would never have done on his own initiative, he suggests, without her seductive blandishments. On the other hand, faced with the knowledge that the society he wants to re-enter will condemn his love for Manon as unworthy of him, he needs to build an image of her which will prove that she was, after all, a worthy object of love. The process can be seen in his account of one of his frequent, but invariably brief bursts of bad conscience, inspired in this instance by Tiberge's financial generosity:

> J'en fus touché, jusqu'au point de déplorer l'aveuglement d'un amour fatal qui me faisait violer tous les devoirs. La vertu eut assez de force pendant quelques moments pour s'élever dans mon cœur contre ma passion, et j'aperçus du moins, dans cet instant de lumière, la honte et l'indignité de mes chaînes. Mais ce combat fut léger et dura peu. La vue de Manon m'aurait fait précipiter du ciel, et je m'étonnai, en me retrouvant près d'elle, que j'eusse pu traiter un moment de honteuse une tendresse si juste pour un objet si charmant. (p.64)

At this moment when society's vision of his love threatens to impose itself on him, he justifies his fidelity to Manon in terms of a 'tendresse juste'; she deserves his love, and fidelity to such a one can thus be seen in the heroic light he desires, even if it is unorthodox in social terms.

Des Grieux, as he tells his story, is thus requiring Manon to serve at the same time as degrading siren and ennobling ideal. It is not implausible, of course, for a passionate and demanding man to make his woman serve as both angel and whore, but it does create tensions, both for the woman, who, as I shall shortly show, has difficulties in combining the two roles, and for the narrator, who has to weld this sharply polarized vision into a convincing character portrayal. The whole enigma of Manon is created by the difficulty of this latter process. Des Grieux solves it, insofar as he does solve it, by presenting an evolving image of Manon; if we follow his statements on her through the novel in the order in which they appear, a clear pattern of idealization emerges.

The first attempt Des Grieux makes to form a judgment on Manon follows the Chaillot fire, and it is harsh:

> Je connaissais Manon; je n'avais déjà que trop éprouvé que, quelque fidèle et quelque attachée qu'elle me fût dans la bonne fortune, il ne fallait pas compter sur elle dans la misère. Elle aimait trop l'abondance et les plaisirs pour me les sacrifier. (p.58)

The implication here is that Manon puts prosperity first and him second, and it is easy to see from her behaviour so far in the story why he should reach this conclusion, but it is not a palatable one, and his next reflection begins to qualify it:

> Manon était une créature d'un caractère extraordinaire. Jamais fille n'eut moins d'attachement qu'elle pour l'argent, mais elle ne pouvait être tranquille un moment, avec la crainte d'en manquer. C'était du plaisir et des passe-temps qu'il lui fallait. Elle n'eût jamais voulu toucher un sou, si l'on pouvait se divertir sans qu'il en coûte. (p.64)

According to this, it is the 'plaisirs' rather than the 'abondance' which count, and the qualification is greatly in her favour as it removes from her any suspicion of mercenary values and the bourgeois vice of avarice. Moreover, Des Grieux is now convinced that he is 'le seul, comme elle en convenait volontiers, qui pût lui faire goûter parfaitement les douceurs de l'amour', and that 'elle m'aurait préféré à toute la terre avec une fortune médiocre' (p.65). He still knows she is likely to leave him in hard times, but at least he is placing more emphasis on the quality of her love for him, and after her escape from the Hôpital, as she renews her vows of fidelity, he finds a new means of explaining away her flightiness:

> J'ai toujours été persuadé qu'elle était sincère; quelle raison aurait-elle eue de se contrefaire jusqu'à ce point? Mais elle était encore plus volage, ou plutôt elle n'était plus rien, et elle ne se reconnaissait pas elle-même, lorsque, ayant devant les yeux des femmes qui vivaient dans l'abondance, elle se trouvait dans la pauvreté et dans le besoin. (p.102)

The proneness to infidelity is still there, but this time he sees it, not as her dominant motive, but as an alienation. Just as he sees himself, in essentialist terms, as a character whose true nature is above the things he does, he has come to recognize in Manon a true nature, which loves him, and relegates the rest to a contingent aberration. He has also discovered in her the crucial quality of sincerity, and this is what saves his image of her at the time of their sharpest quarrel, the one following her escapade with young G... M...:

> ... je fus touché de l'ingénuité de son récit, et de cette manière bonne et ouverte avec laquelle elle me racontait jusqu'aux circonstances dont j'étais le plus offensé. Elle pèche sans malice, disais-je en moi-même; elle est légère et imprudente, mais elle est droite et sincère.
> (p.134)

Her sincerity saves his love for her even after her worst betrayal of him, allowing her fault to appear as childlike irresponsibility rather than anything really culpable, and revealing her as 'droite', a term whose positive ethical connotations become explicit by the time they have reached America and are contemplating marriage: 'Elle était droite et naturelle dans tous ses sentiments, qualité qui dispose toujours à la vertu' (p.166). At last, Des Grieux's image of his beloved can include the unambiguously positive term of 'vertu', just in time to make her death appear edifying.

The pattern behind this series of judgments is unmistakable, an excellent example of how helpful it is, in reading Prévost's novels, to trace the variations in a sequence of repeated situations. With this in mind, it becomes easier to see how Des Grieux wants his audience to interpret Manon. At the beginning, like Des Grieux himself, she is very young, fifteen to his seventeen, more experienced than he, but still a child who does not know herself. Her 'penchant au plaisir' leads her to leave him for a richer man, B..., after their first flight to Paris, but she grieves at having to do so, and it is she who takes the initiative in resuming their relationship when she visits him in Saint-Sulpice, having discovered that she enjoys the pleasures of love more with him than with anyone else. She does not lose her love of pleasure, her irresponsible playfulness or the fear of poverty which causes her to turn to a richer lover in hard times, but after Saint-Sulpice she remains technically faithful to him in that Des Grieux persuades her to forgo her relationship with both the G... M...s before she actually sleeps with them. The two persuasion scenes are very similar, another case of parallel scenes which the author underlines as such (p.126); Des Grieux achieves access to Manon in her abductor's house in advance of the planned betrayal, finds her naïvely pleased to see him, makes her genuinely distressed by showing her how upset he is at the prospect of her sleeping with another man and thus leads her to abandon the idea. This pattern aims to suggest, first, that Manon's infidelity springs from a childlike unawareness of its implications, second, that her love for Des Grieux is, after all, the most important thing for her, and finally, what a clever fellow Des Grieux is to be able to control her in this way. In the end, misfortune matures her, and when they are reunited on the road to Le Havre, Manon is so overwhelmed by the discovery that he actually intends to accompany her to America that she undergoes a conversion, repenting of all her previous disloyalty and transforming her love into something altogether more selfless. On arrival in America, she is allowed to proclaim her *mea culpa* in her own voice, more extensively than usual now that she has something to say that Des Grieux wants us to hear:

> Je sens bien que je n'ai jamais mérité ce prodigieux attachement que vous avez pour moi. Je vous ai causé des chagrins, que vous n'avez pu me pardonner sans une bonté extrême. J'ai été légère et volage, et même en vous aimant éperdument, comme j'ai toujours fait, je n'étais qu'une ingrate. Mais vous ne sauriez croire combien je suis changée. Mes larmes, que vous avez vues couler si souvent depuis notre départ de France, n'ont pas eu une seule fois mes malheurs pour objet. J'ai cessé de les sentir aussitôt que vous avez commencé à les partager. Je n'ai pleuré que de tendresse et de compassion pour vous. (p.165)

This edifying outburst of high-flown sentiment proves to Des Grieux that Manon has, in effect, become herself; the true Manon, faithful lover of Des Grieux, has emerged from her chrysalis, to soar and die in his arms in that brief hour of harmony in the American wilderness which sets the seal on the image of her that Des Grieux wishes to retain.

This image is, however, merely Des Grieux's linguistic construct, and Prévost warns us subtly, at the height of Manon's death scene, that language can obscure communication:

> ... elle me dit, d'une voix faible, qu'elle se croyait à sa dernière heure. Je ne pris d'abord ce discours que pour un langage ordinaire dans l'infortune, et je n'y répondis que par les tendres consolations de l'amour. Mais, ses soupirs fréquents, son silence à mes interrogations, le serrement de ses mains, dans lesquelles elle continuait

> de tenir les miennes me firent connaître que la fin de ses
> malheurs approchait. (p.174)

Accustomed as he is to the superlatives and hyperboles of the
emotive vocabulary of his age, he does not at first take Manon's
claim to be at her 'last hour' as the literal truth. It is a note of
disharmony, clashing with the general impression he seeks to give
at this point of two souls functioning on the same wavelength, and it
signals the possibility that Des Grieux's understanding of his
beloved is far from complete.

   This does not prevent critics who try to fill in the gaps from
finding themselves on dangerous ground. With her air of childlike
naturalness and her closeness to common roots, Manon tends to
appear to critics as basically a simple girl made problematic chiefly
by Des Grieux's vision of her, but the attempts made to penetrate
beyond his vision are so lacking in consensus that she comes to look
far from simple. There are two schools of thought on Manon, one
making her appear worse than Des Grieux suggests, the other
suggesting that she is not so bad. The first, of which Germain is the
main modern advocate (*16*), builds on the undoubted skill as a liar
which Manon demonstrates in the text and argues that she uses it to
deceive Des Grieux. According to this theory, the 'vieil Argus'
escorting her on their first meeting (p.32) is in fact a lover with
whom she has eloped rather than a loyal family retainer, and a
strong case is made that she could have slept with both G... M...s.
The evidence on which this is based is circumstantial, raising
suspicions again that if Prévost had really meant to signal this
interpretation, he would have found clearer ways of doing it, but it
is persuasively argued and a nagging reminder that with a
dissembler like Manon, anything is possible. Germain's case is
limited by its lack of any reference to her conversion in the closing
stages, but this too can be called in question by the cynical. I
occasionally ask groups of students how they think Manon would
have reacted if the rival lover confronting her in America had not
been Synnelet, a man of merely local importance, but a rich trader
generous enough to offer Manon a passage back to Europe and

foolish enough to take Des Grieux as well. The pursuit of might-have-beens is no doubt frivolous and misleading, and my question is no doubt loaded, but it is striking that the vast majority think that Manon would have accepted the deal. At the very least this suggests that if Prévost had meant to make Manon's conversion convincing, he has not been altogether successful. As so often with this pair of lovers, an aura of ambiguity prevails.

It is worth noting in passing how the Italian prince episode, inserted in the 1753 edition, heightens that ambiguity. Its explicit aim is to fill out the portrayal of Manon, but the filling out does not necessarily imply clarification. It portrays Manon making a show of rejecting a rich lover at a time when their fortune is moderately well established, thus authenticating her love for Des Grieux and providing him with the evidence necessary to support his judgment, expressed prior to the involvement with young G... M..., that 'Manon ... ne pouvait supporter le nom de la pauvreté. Cependant, ... lorsqu'il n'est question que du plus ou du moins, je ne la crois pas capable de m'abandonner pour un autre' (pp.117–18). Since there is no other evidence in the story so far which points very clearly towards that conclusion, the Italian prince episode has its value; it also reinforces the irresponsible playfulness of her character, and shows the control she exercises over Des Grieux in the scene where she persuades him to stay at home and let his hair be arranged as if he were a woman. Yet any impression we have of knowing Manon better from this scene is immediately counteracted by her escapade with young G... M... Des Grieux's financial fortune is just the same during this escapade as it was during the Italian prince episode, yet Manon decides to accept offers which she had rejected from the Italian prince. There are signs that Manon is seriously tempted to leave Des Grieux for young G... M..., the only one so far of Des Grieux's rivals to be young and potentially attractive. Her long explanation to Des Grieux of her behaviour with young G... M..., a statement which Des Grieux describes as 'droite et sincère' (p.134), is in fact distinctly shifty over the matter of the girl she sends to him as a substitute, and even if she is telling the truth about the matter to Des Grieux, she proves what a good liar she is in what she admits to having said to young G... M... Seen as a prelude to this most ambivalent of Manon's betrayals, the Italian prince episode points to a discontinuity in Manon's character and raises more problems than it solves.

The majority of recent interpretations of Manon, however, tend in the opposite direction, finding reasons to excuse the worst parts of Manon's behaviour and to emphasize the genuineness of her attraction to Des Grieux. It is possible, for instance, to see Manon, as Coulet does, as a figure analogous to Mary Magdalene, a repentant sinner with a capacity for sacrifice corresponding to what Des Grieux wants the reader to see in himself (7). Without necessarily going as far as this, many critics defend Manon on the grounds that she is a victim, both of society in general and of Des Grieux in particular. It is easy to show, as Delesalle and Singerman have done (9, 32), that a lower-class woman like Manon can expect little justice from society. Des Grieux, a man and an aristocrat, can use his influence to be released from prison for the same crimes that cause Manon to be transported to America with no possibility of appeal. A woman once fallen has no chance of recovering social esteem; even Lescaut admits that, 'sa sœur ayant une fois violé les lois de son sexe, ... il ne s'était réconcilié avec elle que dans l'espérance de tirer parti de sa mauvaise conduite' (p.60). Given that Manon has sinned against the strictest standards of sexual morality, society makes it very hard for her to do anything but continue along the same road, and it is possible to interpret Manon's infidelity as a realistic and practical reaction to that situation. Put bluntly, her only choice is between being a high-class prostitute and a low-class prostitute, and as a girl of spirit it is not surprising that she should aim at the former by cultivating rich lovers. Such a course would not preclude her, under the mores of the age, from keeping Des Grieux as a favoured lover, or 'greluchon', sharing her favours and her profits. As she says to Des Grieux, 'la fidélité que je souhaite de vous est celle du cœur' (p.133), implying that this can be distinguished from physical fidelity; this is why she has no qualms at sending him a substitute girl while she is with young G... M... Seen in this light, a coherent explanation of her behaviour becomes possible. She loves Des Grieux genuinely and her infidelities are not betrayals, since her heart is not involved, simply business arrangements of which she means to share the profit with her impecunious true love. Ignoble this may be, but according to her lights it is acceptable and workable, nor is it without appeal to some aspects of twentieth-century sexual mores, with its emphasis on the woman's freedom and responsibility and its refusal to consider certain types of infidelity as irredeemable stains. It is even possible to present Manon, as Gasster has done (*15*), in terms suggesting that she is the prototype of the modern emancipated businesswoman.

The trouble is that Des Grieux will not accept the role of 'greluchon'. An aristocrat with lofty notions of sacrifice and shedding his blood in noble causes, he is not at home in the world of business calculations, especially in sexual matters, and when Manon goes off to G... M..., leaving him a letter explaining that she is doing it for him and for their greater prosperity, his reaction is furious:

> Elle appréhende la faim. Dieu d'amour! quelle grossièreté de sentiments! et que c'est répondre mal à ma délicatesse! Je ne l'ai pas appréhendée, moi qui m'y expose si volontiers pour elle en renonçant à ma fortune et aux douceurs de la maison de mon père; moi qui me suis retranché jusqu'au nécessaire pour satisfaire ses petites humeurs et ses caprices. (p.70)

Nowhere does Des Grieux underline more sharply what separates his noble self from his plebeian mistress. He has made sacrifices for her, and he expects her to do the same for him, to respond in the noble vein to which he is accustomed. What he does not realize is the consequences of the sacrifices he asks. He himself has never been seriously at risk from anything he does; there is always the safety net of his family to fall back on in a real crisis, and his appeal to his father after his second imprisonment shows that he knows it. She fears poverty more than anything else, and with good reason; a lover capable of supporting her is all that stands between her and utter ruin, and her decision to accept G... M...'s offers is, from her own point of view, totally logical. She has a choice, in effect, between two life-styles, love in a garret with Des Grieux or a prosperous *ménage à trois*; she would prefer the latter, but Des Grieux, stepping in to reclaim her before she concludes matters with G... M..., insists on the former without showing much sign of thinking through the implications. The result is an unsustainable compromise; they take G... M...'s money but refuse to pay the sexual price, and they end up in prison, a pattern which is repeated in its essentials later in the novel with G... M...'s son.

It now becomes clear how Manon is Des Grieux's victim. They love each other, but in different ways, Des Grieux's noble but impractical, Manon's base but realistic, and the plot is engendered by the tension between the two. It is Manon who appears to dominate the relationship at first, to wheedle Des Grieux into doing things the way she wants, but as the story progresses, Des Grieux imposes his will more and more, and by forcing Manon to take decisions going against her practical interests, it is he who brings her to the disaster of her transportation to America. If this is so, her conversion on the way to America appears less like a dramatic rupture with her past than a step in an ongoing process, and at the same time it loses some of the noble sacrificial quality that Des Grieux tries to read into it. By agreeing to accompany her to America, Des Grieux has become her irreplaceable sole support, and she is forced to see things his way, if only in her own interests, which means that all her claims to love Des Grieux with a new selflessness could be interpreted merely as the steps she needs to take to bind him to her as closely as possible. Moreover, these claims are accompanied by signs that her own individual personality has been weakened. In the departure port of Le Havre, she expresses a wish for death which contrasts strikingly with the vitality she has shown earlier on (p.161), and her actual death, of which the cause is nothing more arduous than a five-mile walk into the wilderness and a night in the open, seems to come remarkably quickly, especially in comparison with Fanny, heroine of *Cleveland*, who in even more harrowing circumstances treks for thousands of miles across

America and survives. It is as if Des Grieux has imposed an alien personality on Manon which, quite apart from forcing her into life-destroying circumstances, has deprived her of the will to live.

Such an interpretation would be fully consonant with the facts of the story as Des Grieux presents them, and it is hardly surprising that he does not arrive at it himself, since it would undermine the image of Manon that he wants to build and would show his own role in a distinctly unattractive light. Prévost himself, however, may well have been thinking along these lines. Space does not permit a comparative study of the feminine figures in Prévost's novels, which I have already attempted in another work (*14*, pp.205–224), but when viewed in their context, this interpretation of Manon looks even more sustainable. Prévost was no feminist in the modern sense of the word; he regards women as the weaker sex, governed by emotions, highly impressionable and with a dangerous tendency to passivity which leaves them as putty in the hands of their more decisive male lovers. Yet he sympathized with women's lot, as did many eighteenth-century novelists, and his works highlight the many ways in which society and egocentric male passion make women eternal victims. Most of the heroines of the *Mémoires d'un homme de qualité* are driven by these forces either to death or to retreat from the world. Naomi Segal, in the leading feminist inter-pretation of *Manon Lescaut* (*27*), has shown how Des Grieux as he speaks to Renoncour is speaking the language of males which tends to exclude women, but that does not mean that Prévost's own vision is limited to a narrowly male perspective. Because men are stronger than women, he would argue, it is man's responsibility to protect women and help them overcome their impressionability to live according to their own best values. Yet men too are weak, and the result is that their passions drag women down instead of supporting them, especially in a society which pays little attention to strength-ening women's character through a good education. A common pattern in Prévost's novels is for a poorly educated woman to fall under the influence of a friend or lover who tries to subject her to a second, more noble education, but can never completely suc-ceed, partly because a bad initial education can never be entirely eradicated, partly because of women's inherent passivity and partly because of the inadequacies of the tutor-lover. Julie in *Le Doyen de Killerine*, Théophé in the *Histoire d'une Grecque moderne* and Mlle de Créon in *Le Monde moral* are examples of the type, and Manon would fit well within it, trapped as she is between her base family and Des Grieux. She also compares interestingly with Fanny in *Cleveland*, who sacrifices her own personality to an excessive degree in an attempt to conform to the pattern of wifely behaviour which she thinks her husband requires of her. Manon is part of the tragic picture Prévost paints of women's attempts to find a place in a man's world, attempts which he seems to think are doomed to failure. The reduction of Manon from a fun-loving young girl to a shadowy function in the discourse of an unenlightened male is an apt way of expressing this tragic vision.

5. Value-Systems

So far in this study I have tried to show how this novel can best be read in order to make sense of the material it presents. In this chapter I shall take a closer look at some of the issues raised, and attempt to see what kind of a statement it is, if any, that Prévost is trying to make. I have said nothing so far about the author himself, in deliberate reaction against a school of criticism which for many years sought to explain *Manon Lescaut* in narrowly autobiographical terms. Sgard's researches (30), by creating a balanced picture of the relationship between Prévost's art and his life, have done much to correct this overemphasis, and readers who wish to explore Prévost's biography should turn to his work. It would, however, be useful to begin by glancing briefly at some of the themes and attitudes to which Prévost's turbulent life inclined him.

There is no reason to assume, as did earlier biographers like Harrisse (20), that *Manon Lescaut* tells the story of Prévost's adventures before he became a monk, but it is known that the young Prévost took monastic vows, with little sense of vocation, after a love-affair turned sour, and that after eight uneasy years he walked out of his monastery. When *Manon Lescaut* was published in 1731, he was living in exile in Holland, short of cash, apparently emerging from another unhappy love-affair in England and possibly already longing for the return to a respectable position in France which some years later he was able to negotiate. With this background, it is not surprising that he should take an interest in the theme of passion and the difficulty of controlling it. One of the nagging questions running through all his fiction is whether the mind and the will have the force to protect a man from the alienating disorders which passion entails. The orthodox Renoncour claims that they do, but it is likely that Prévost shares Des Grieux's doubts on the matter. Prévost's history also draws him to the theme of commitment; having taken monastic vows and broken them, he is fascinated by characters who are unable to live within their own self-imposed value-systems and he admires those who can achieve constancy in whatever shape or form. Prévost's ecclesiastical training is likely to have left him with a serious interest in moral problems, even when he knows he cannot solve them, and his position as a reluctant exile is likely to incline him against controversial stances which might impede his rehabilitation. There is much evidence that Prévost was a conciliator by nature; the title of his periodical, *Le Pour et Contre*, reflects his eagerness to be fair to both sides of a question, and his constant need to placate the ecclesiastical and political authorities led him to tailor his writings according to what he thought would be safe and acceptable. This makes him an elusive, even rather a shifty figure, difficult to pin down in ideological terms, but it equips him well for the writing of fiction, in which it is more important to express ideological conflicts in human terms than to find neat intellectual resolutions.

Manon Lescaut can be interpreted as a three-cornered conflict within Des Grieux between opposing but overlapping value-systems, a code of strict religious conformism, the code of honourable behaviour accepted in aristocratic society and a code whereby love justifies all. I have already shown how Des Grieux resolves it; though never denying the values embodied in the first two codes and doing his best to avoid rupture for as long as possible, he cannot in the end live according to them and therefore tries to make a virtue out of the commitment he shows to the third. In this chapter I shall proceed by examining these value-systems in turn, to see how coherent Prévost makes them look.

The code which argues the supremacy of love seems at first sight the least open to intellectual formulation, but it can be described in terms of the eighteenth-century phenomenon of sensibility, which has been usefully discussed in the context of this novel by Vivienne Mylne (*24*, pp.32 ff.). Prévost was one of the earliest writers to bring together the elements of this phenomenon, a mood rather than a theory, in which a capacity for emotion is taken to demonstrate the extent of the soul and to go alongside a capacity for merit and virtue. It is this extent which Des Grieux is claiming for himself in his celebrated tirade on his entry into Saint-Lazare, in which he asserts that he is part of an élite feeling more emotions than the average man:

> Le commun des hommes n'est sensible qu'à cinq ou six passions, dans le cercle desquelles leur vie se passe, et où toutes leurs agitations se réduisent. Otez-leur l'amour et la haine, le plaisir et la douleur, l'espérance et la crainte, ils ne sentent plus rien. Mais les personnes d'un caractère plus noble peuvent être remuées de mille façons différentes; il semble qu'elles aient plus de cinq sens, et qu'elles puissent recevoir des idées et des sensations qui passent les bornes ordinaires de la nature; et comme elles ont un sentiment de cette grandeur qui les élève au-dessus du vulgaire, il n'y a rien dont elles soient plus jalouses. (p.79)

This passage is full of the language of nobility; Des Grieux is claiming to participate in an aristocracy of the soul, which, for various reasons of education levels and social refinement, is always likely to correspond closely to the social élite to which he is also proud to belong. Certainly it suits his narratorial strategy to blur any distinction there may be between the two. Significantly, the emotion which inspires this statement is not his feeling for Manon, but the characteristically aristocratic sense of shame inspired by the discovery that his misdeeds are public knowledge.

Under such a code of values, it is obviously in one's interests to demonstrate one's superiority by allowing emotions to show. One of the biggest difficulties that modern readers face with the literature of sensibility is the need to take seriously the copious tears, swoons and embraces, indulged in by even the more virile males, which were so much more acceptable in eighteenth-century mores than they are now. Des Grieux's emotivity, however, is extreme even by eighteenth-century standards. The reaction to bad news, for instance, is one of the yardsticks by which Prévost allows his characters' strength of feeling to be measured, and there is nothing in any of his novels to surpass Des Grieux's violent outburst when G... M... tells him that Manon is in the Hôpital:

> Quand j'aurais eu une prison éternelle, ou la mort même présente à mes yeux, je n'aurais pas été le maître de mon transport, à cette affreuse nouvelle. Je me jetai sur lui avec une si furieuse rage que j'en perdis la moitié de mes forces. J'en eus assez néanmoins pour le renverser par terre, et pour le prendre à la gorge... O Dieu! m'écriai-je, en poussant mille soupirs; justice du Ciel! faut-il que je vive un moment, après une telle infamie? Je voulus me jeter encore sur le barbare qui venait de m'assassiner. On m'arrêta. Mon désespoir, mes cris et mes larmes passaient toute imagination. Je fis des choses si étonnantes, que tous les assistants, qui en ignoraient la cause, se regardaient les uns les autres avec autant de frayeur que de surprise. (p.82)

Here again, Des Grieux the aristocrat is to the fore, incensed by the 'infamie' of his mistress being in so base a place and, for the reader's benefit, wishing to counteract the naming of this place with a display of high-flown sentiment. Clearly his description of his reaction, inflated as it is with lofty-sounding rhetoric, is meant to impress the reader by demonstrating his capacity for emotion.

Yet on closer inspection it looks too neatly and theatrically arranged. Given his supposedly weakened and incoherent state, the words flow a trifle too freely, and his lucid perception of the onlookers' reaction raises a suspicion that some of it is done for effect. A passage such as this, at the same time as it proves his sensibility, can also be classed as part of the process I have described in an earlier chapter of giving Des Grieux the rope with which to hang himself; the reader may well conclude that this is an ill-judged burst of adolescent hysteria rather than righteous noble wrath. So it is with many of the emotional scenes which Des Grieux acts out in this work; the author has enough sympathy with the sufferings of the passionate to let Des Grieux have his head and make as effective a case for himself as possible, but retains a critical eye for the exaggerations and misdeeds that passion inspires and portrays them in such a way as to leave the reader uneasy. One should not assume that Prévost fully agrees with his narrator that the code of values implied by a cult of emotion is enough to impart unambiguous heroic stature.

As far as one can judge from his other writings, Prévost is prepared to privilege love among the human passions, in that it is less selfish and material than others, such as ambition or avarice, but he does not agree that love is inevitably ennobling. Renoncour (2, p.122) and most of his soberer narrators agree that love is morally neutral, ennobling or degrading according to the quality of the object. This of course, in Des Grieux's case, shifts the problem back to whether or not one thinks Manon a worthy object of love, which is a very open question. Another clue lies in Prévost's attitude to nature, which unfortunately does not emerge fully in *Manon Lescaut*. In *Cleveland*, however, the hero grounds the lover's claims to his own code of values firmly in the laws of nature. This at first sight appears well in line with the cult of nature which characterized much Enlightenment thought, but it is not a cult which Prévost himself shares. Des Grieux, it is true, bases Manon's claim to virtue in the fact that she is 'droite et naturelle' (p.166), and on the way to America he toys with the image of the simple savages he will meet there, among whom it will be far more possible for two lovers to live in peace than it would be in French society:

[Les sauvages] nous laisseront du moins vivre en paix.
Si les relations qu'on en fait sont fidèles, ils suivent les
lois de la nature. Ils ne connaissent ni les fureurs de
l'avarice, qui possèdent G... M..., ni les idées
fantastiques de l'honneur, qui m'ont fait un ennemi de
mon père. Ils ne troubleront point deux amants qu'ils
verront vivre avec autant de simplicité qu'eux. (p.160)

If such savages exist, however, Des Grieux never finds them, only remote outposts of all the evils of society. Even Cleveland's more extensive experience of American savages is profoundly ambivalent; nature means cannibals as well as ideal innocence, and the conclusion seems to be that nature in itself is not enough. It offers freedom from certain corruptions, but to achieve true merit it needs to be refined by reason, the right kind of social organization and divine grace. Whatever nostalgic appeal Prévost may find in the idea of a value-system based entirely on the excellence of nature, love and sentiment, he never allows it to pass unchallenged; the laws of God and society have legitimate claims which must not be flouted. At the same time, such a value-system has enough attractive qualities to highlight deficiencies in the laws of God and society, and there is some evidence that Des Grieux is using it as a stick with which to beat the other two codes.

We have seen that, if forced to choose between his religious or his aristocratic status, Des Grieux would probably choose the latter. He is of noble family, and his language shows him anxious to be seen to uphold the noble code of honour based on family pride, generosity, loyalty in friendship and willingness to shed his blood in a noble cause, values which take their origin both in the aristocracy's traditional military role in society and in a long literary tradition descending from the age of chivalry through Corneille and the seventeenth-century novel. I have already shown how, despite everything, Des Grieux is willing to sacrifice these values for Manon's sake; the point I now wish to make is that his story shows the aristocratic code itself under threat from changing social pressures.

The code of the aristocrat is rooted in the traditional hierarchical society associated with the great European monarchies, and as Sgard has pointed out (*31*, pp.47 ff.), Prévost sets his novel plots against a background of declining monarchies, in an age in which the older social structures have lost something of their moral authority. *Manon Lescaut* is no exception. Critics have traditionally assumed that the work is set in the Regency, that period of dissolution, social change and experimentation which followed the death of Louis XIV, but it has now been shown by Sgard (*31*, pp.56 ff.) that the novel's internal chronology is much more coherent if it is assumed to take place a few years earlier, just before Louis XIV's death, at a time when the old structures are still in place with their full authoritarian weight, but already confronting rising forces which will soon be challenging them and which the reader of the 1730s could with hindsight readily perceive to be already at work in the novel. This has the effect of enhancing the drama of Des Grieux's battle against the established forces of his generation. In the Regency, he would have been part of a well-established social trend; five years earlier, his role is rather that of a lonely rebel.

The main rising forces of the Regency were the tendencies to unruliness and sexual and religious laxity which were to burst forth in the changed mood of Philippe of Orleans's court, and above all the newly emerging moneyed classes who were increasingly to challenge and destabilize the old social hierarchy, especially at the time of the financial crisis sparked off by the policies of John Law. Des Grieux is part of the first of these forces, but the second is his adversary; among his rivals for Manon, B... certainly, and probably also G... M..., are men who owe their influence to new money. Such men were not popular in society; they were financiers and tax farmers, the source of their wealth was often suspect and there was no love lost between them and an often impecunious old nobility who rightly felt threatened by these upstarts. Des Grieux's father has no respect for B..., significantly refusing to add the particle of nobility to his name, and Des Grieux himself taunts G... M... with the claim that 'je suis d'un sang plus noble et plus pur que le tien' (p.138).

The presence of such men at the heart of the story leads to one of the most original features of this work, its treatment of the theme of money. Previously, this had been a subject beneath the notice of any writer whose characters had any claim to nobility, heroism or refined sentiment; it might have a place in burlesque novels, but in more serious work the hero was supposed to carry out his great deeds without drawing attention to any enabling finance, or lack of it. In *Manon Lescaut*, the coins are counted, and often with considerable precision. This contributes greatly to the impression of realism given by the work, but the constant emphasis on such an ignoble subject and on Des Grieux's need to live in a world dominated by it serves to undermine something of the heroic image he seeks to cultivate.

In another sense, however, he needs this world as a backdrop to his predicament. As a devotee, however half-hearted, of the old code of honour, he hopes that he will command the reader's sympathy in his fight against the new unpopular moneyed class, which embodies no values higher than the bourgeois vice of avarice and whose unprincipled behaviour is amply illustrated in the story. He hopes to be seen as a representative of traditional virtues and a more attractive social type whose lapses may therefore be forgiven; however bad he is, he suggests, he is not as irredeemably base as his adversaries. It helps him in this bid for sympathy that he is fighting a losing battle; he, a poor and isolated noble youth, can do so little against a rising social force whose weapons are so much more powerful than his. As an aristocrat, his own preferred weapon would be the sword, but he cannot use the sword on rivals who settle their differences by manipulating the forces of the law. Only once does he have the chance to confront a rival in the traditional aristocratic way, that of fighting a duel. Synnelet, his Louisiana rival, is the adversary concerned, and it is important to his image of himself that he conducts this duel exemplarily, making the classic noble gesture of returning his opponent's sword after disarming him. 'Un sang généreux ne se dément jamais', he loftily reflects (p.171). As well as being the one place, far from social realities, which might give him the chance to live out his role as an ideal lover, Louisiana also allows him to play a role of ideal nobility, and perhaps more successfully. It is significant that, after Manon's death, the two swordsmen develop a respect for each other.

For the bulk of the novel, however, Des Grieux can do little more than deploy the rhetoric of shedding his blood valiantly without ever being called upon to do so. As the cowardly Lescaut knows, the age of duelling is past, Louis XIV's government having taken strict measures to suppress it, and the incongruity of Des Grieux's rhetoric with the prevailing social mood makes his words look hollow and his values irrelevant. Moreover, there are serious flaws in the code of honour itself, and Des Grieux's conflict with the authorities helps to highlight them. His father is, of course, the novel's main representative of aristocratic values, and his behaviour towards his son's passion shows the code's strengths and weaknesses. An affectionate father, he is indulgent towards his son, more willing than many of his class would be to change his plans to suit his son's inclinations. Initially he shows cynical amusement rather than moral outrage at the affair with Manon; as long as it can be seen as an inconsequential sowing of wild oats he is not unduly worried, less so than Tiberge with his religious concern for the salvation of a sinner. This already points to a limitation in his values, which seem a little short on moral content. In the central story of the *Mémoires*, Rosemont's father shows the same limitation to an even greater degree by his willingness to countenance a secret marriage for his son, provided it can later be broken in favour of a proper dynastic marriage. Neither father takes emotion seriously, and neither regards the woman concerned as anything other than an expendable pawn; Des Grieux's father ultimately shows it by arranging for Manon's deportation and thus provoking his son to open revolt. By this act he shows the authoritarian basis of the aristocratic code. Its main concern is the preservation of the family, and, to avoid a dishonouring *mésalliance*, underlings and women can be dismissed without consideration or scruple. Conformity to social expectations rather than generosity seems to be the essential value, and, if so, the quality of the code of honour seems diminished.

This concern for conformism can ultimately degenerate into the elevation of public image above all else; any substantial values embodied by the code become swamped by the cult of appearances. Prévost explores this theme more tellingly in his later novels than he does in *Manon Lescaut*, but something of the process can be seen in the role played by M. de T... I have already suggested that his relationship with Des Grieux is a parody of noble friendship, and that his influence on Des Grieux is harmful. A pleasure-loving youth with as irresponsible an eye for a frivolous scheme as Manon

herself, he shows few signs of nobility in his behaviour, and its
limits are clearly shown in his final meeting with Des Grieux. It is
M. de T... who suggests to him the plan of rescuing Manon on the
road to transportation with the aid of hired thugs, a form of violence
which falls distinctly short of duelling in terms of nobility, and M.
de T... clearly knows it, for he will not dirty his hands in the process
himself: 'Il ajouta que, si le soin de sa réputation lui eût permis
d'entreprendre lui-même la délivrance de ma maîtresse, il m'eût
offert son bras et son épée' (p.151). This proposal of an ignoble
scheme from which its author keeps himself at arm's length seems
to fall short of the 'excessive générosité' that Des Grieux sees in it.
The assumption seems to be that a noble's first duty is to keep his
reputation intact rather than help a friend in distress; image is more
important than substance. Des Grieux himself is fully aware of the
importance of appearances, having earlier exploited his own
appearance of being an honest young noble to make a career out of
card-sharping. Modern readers often ask why Des Grieux cannot
simply find a job to support his mistress rather than resorting to this
kind of swindle; the explanation is that aristocratic prejudices
against trade and other moneymaking activities were such that he
may well have run more risk of derogation, or loss of aristocratic
privileges, by taking a job than he would have done by being caught
cheating at cards. Here again, concern for conforming to the behaviour patterns of his class leads to a course of action which by other
standards might be perceived as immoral.

The emerging vision of society is gloomy indeed, a world of
criminality and deception in which a harsh emergent capitalism
confronts an ageing and decadent hierarchy, in which the vices of
the old and the licentious constantly restrict the hardly more virtuous young, and in which the individual has little chance of obtain-
ing justice, especially if she is a woman of the lower orders. Against
this background, it is easy for Des Grieux to project an image of two
basically innocent lovers dragged down by their social environment;
whether or not one accepts their innocence, many readers will allow
that they are superior to their surroundings. If so, it raises the
question of whether Prévost intended this to be a work of social

criticism. Certainly the elements are there, and it would not be difficult to find in Prévost the same kind of concerns as were voiced by his contemporaries, Montesquieu and Voltaire. Yet it is dangerous to use historical hindsight to annex Prévost too firmly to the Enlightenment. Nowhere does he express any positive vision of what he thinks society should be. His pessimistic view of human nature is more akin to seventeenth-century classicism and theology than to Enlightenment values, and he seems to have regarded the flaws of society as inevitable consequences of the flaws of human nature, with little hope of putting them right. In any case, his avoidance of controversial issues would tend to lead him away from too pointed a comment on the evils of society. The fact that *Manon Lescaut* was actually banned on its first appearance in France owing to its portrayal of lax moral standards in high places shows how careful he had to be. The social vision in this work is best viewed as tragic in character; its evils are portrayed in a mode of lucid resignation, with no combative aim of improvement.

Prévost had to be even more careful in his handling of religious themes. Having spent most of his adult life steering a delicate course between Jesuits, Jansenists, Benedictines and the Protestants among whom he was living when *Manon Lescaut* was published, he well knew how any religious statement he made would be open to subtle interpretation designed to prove or disprove sectarian allegiances which he usually preferred to leave unclear. Yet by the same token he knew how to let his narrator make teasing religious allusions which suggest more than they reveal. In one of the most important recent contributions to our understanding of Prévost's intellectual life, Singerman (*33*) has demonstrated how Prévost's profound roots in the Augustinian theology of the seventeenth century have found expression in a language and a series of allusions which permeate the whole novel. Whether this makes Prévost a theologian is another matter.

We have seen that the narrating Des Grieux claims to have been touched by grace, but this does not prevent him from hinting that his God has done too little for him, and done it too late. For a start, divine grace has not protected him from falling in love in the first place. He does not explicitly blame Providence for causing his passion; the supernatural force he actually invokes is described in pagan or astrological terms as 'l'ascendant de ma destinée qui m'entraînait à ma perte' (p.32). Like most of Prévost's narrators, he maintains a careful separation between the pagan language of fatality and the Christian language of Providence, preferring the former when expressing notions of the supernatural which are not easily encompassed by Christian orthodoxy. Nor, however, does he share the view of the orthodox Renoncour that divine grace is always available to help those who sincerely want to fight against passion (2, p.175). To Tiberge, he presents his love as 'un de ces coups particuliers du destin qui s'attache à la ruine d'un misérable, et dont il est aussi impossible à la vertu de se défendre qu'il l'a été à la sagesse de les prévoir' (p.63), and later to the same audience, his rhetorical question: 'De quels secours n'aurais-je pas besoin pour oublier les charmes de Manon?' (p.89) clearly hints that the necessary help from Heaven has not been forthcoming. The ensuing exchange, in which Des Grieux neither confirms nor denies Tiberge's accusation of Jansenism, has caused much ink to be spilt. The context of the debate is, of course, the bitter and highly politicized doctrinal conflict between the Jansenists and the Jesuits which dominated the French church in the first decades of the eighteenth century, and which did not cease with the official condemnation of Jansenism. The availability or non-availability of divine grace was one of the main points at issue in this conflict, with the Jansenists taking the harsh view, akin to Calvinist notions of predestination, that grace is available only to a chosen few and that man cannot attract grace to himself by his actions. It is easy to see how Des Grieux can exploit this concept of grace to make himself appear an innocent victim in the eyes of the theologically aware Tiberge, but to use his allusion to claim that Des Grieux, and *a fortiori* Prévost, are Jansenists is to go too far; Prévost would not wish to commit himself, and Des Grieux's interests lie elsewhere. For the young narrator, it is simply a matter of giving himself extra dignity through a modish theological vocabulary, by presenting his misdeeds in the context of a widespread, semi-respectable heretical school, rather than as a purely anarchic individual revolt. His pessimism on the subject of grace stays with him even as he narrates, however, at a time when grace is supposed after all to have come to him. The following reflection immediately precedes the return of his passion when Manon visits him in Saint-Sulpice:

> S'il est vrai que les secours célestes sont à tous moments d'une force égale à celle des passions, qu'on m'explique donc par quel funeste ascendant on se trouve emporté tout d'un coup loin de son devoir, sans se trouver capable de la moindre résistance, et sans ressentir le moindre remords. (p.50)

The importance of these words is that they are clearly the expression of his thoughts as narrator rather than at the time of events, and if he can still think this way as he tells his story, it suggests that he is still confused over the whole issue of grace and the ability to resist passion, perhaps indeed that his claim to be in a state of grace at the end is merely an empty gesture. Orthodoxy has still not conquered him.

God has also shown hostility to him, Des Grieux argues, in the manner of Manon's death. This he regards as a punishment from God, and he is submissive enough to accept that as a sinner he deserves his punishment. What incenses him is the way this punishment comes, as a direct result of his desire to return to virtue by marrying Manon:

> Je suis persuadé qu'il n'y a point d'honnête homme au monde qui n'eût approuvé mes vues dans les circon-stances où j'étais... Mais se trouvera-t-il quelqu'un qui accuse mes plaintes d'injustice, si je gémis de la rigueur du Ciel à rejeter un dessein que je n'avais formé que pour lui plaire? Hélas! que dis-je, à le rejeter? Il l'a puni comme un crime. Il m'avait souffert avec patience tandis que je marchais aveuglément dans la route du vice, et ses plus rudes châtiments m'étaient réservés

> lorsque je commençais à retourner à la vertu.
>
> (pp.167–68)

Des Grieux is choosing his terms very carefully, trading on the
ambiguity of the terms 'plaintes' and 'gémir', which in the context
could be taken to mean simply that he is claiming the purely human
right to express his grief at what happened. Yet the other possible
meaning, that he is complaining about the injustice of God, is also
strongly signalled, and it appears that he is once again using his
rhetorical ingenuity to combine a movement of revolt with an
appearance of submission. A similar ambivalent impression arises
in the description of their last night together:

> Je passai la nuit entière à veiller près d'elle, et à prier le
> Ciel de lui accorder un sommeil doux et paisible. O
> Dieu! que mes vœux étaient vifs et sincères! et par quel
> rigoureux jugement aviez-vous résolu de ne les pas
> exaucer! (p.173)

Manon dies against a background of unanswered prayer, and Des
Grieux narrates her death with a touch of indignation at Heaven's
silence.

It appears from all these examples that Des Grieux is allowing
himself to express a significant amount of disrespect for religion,
never enough to cut himself off totally from orthodoxy, but enough
to suggest that he is champing at the bit. Perhaps the most striking
example is the way he abuses religious vocabulary, in his great
debate with Tiberge in Saint-Lazare, to suggest that his love for
Manon is analogous to a religious man's devotion to God:

> J'aime Manon; je tends au travers de mille douleurs à
> vivre heureux et tranquille auprès d'elle. La voie par où
> je marche est malheureuse; mais l'espérance d'arriver à
> mon terme y répand toujours de la douceur, et je me
> croirai trop bien payé, par un moment passé avec elle,
> de tous les chagrins que j'essuie pour l'obtenir. (p.87)

Substitute 'Dieu' for 'Manon' in this virtuoso passage, and it trans-
forms effortlessly into the expression of the sufferings of a saint or
martyr. Like many of the things he says in this debate, it is not
meant to be a serious statement of his thought, but an extreme
position adopted for the sake of argument, from which he subsequently withdraws so as to demonstrate that he is not really as
blasphemous as he appears, but at the same time without losing the
impact of the blasphemy.

Behind these verbal fireworks, we may detect two serious
purposes. First, Des Grieux is trying to suggest that there is a
genuine kinship between his quest for Manon and the believer's
quest for God, in that both involve sacrifice and renunciation of
certain types of worldly goods. One conventionally admires this
renunciation in men of religion, and Des Grieux hints that he
should qualify for some of the same admiration. Secondly, he is
establishing his superiority over Tiberge. I have already suggested
that the kind things Des Grieux makes a point of saying about his
clerical friend are merely lip-service; the picture the story presents
of Des Grieux exploiting Tiberge's good nature and making rings
round him in argument contrasts strikingly with the respect he
shows for his father, symbol of worldly authority. Des Grieux in fact
needs to show Tiberge as a slow-witted creature, slightly out of
touch with reality, because it corresponds to one of his most funda-
mental criticisms of religion and its representatives on earth. This is
how he concludes his case in the Saint-Lazare debate:

> Prédicateurs, qui voulez me ramener à la vertu, dites-
> moi qu'elle est indispensablement nécessaire, mais ne
> me déguisez pas qu'elle est sévère et pénible. Etablissez
> bien que les délices de l'amour sont passagères, qu'elles
> sont défendues, qu'elles seront suivies par d'éternelles
> peines,... mais confessez qu'avec des cœurs tels que
> nous les avons, elles sont ici-bas nos plus parfaites
> félicités. (p.88)

In face of the undoubted psychological fact that sex is fun, he is saying, the church has very little to offer. Its promises seem hollow, its language seems remote from the concerns of real life, and in general it fails to engage seriously with the problems it should be trying to solve. Churchmen appear to inhabit a different world from that of men like Des Grieux, and they have not found an effective means of bridging the gap.

In this respect, Des Grieux comes close to Renoncour's pessimistic observation in the *Avis de l'auteur*, that, 'tous les préceptes de la morale n'étant que des principes vagues et généraux, il est très difficile d'en faire une application particulière au détail des mœurs et des actions' (p.22). The two narrators concur on the difficulty of matching theory to practice, intentions to realizations, and Prévost himself, with his personal history of inconstancy, is likely to agree. The *Avis* tries to go beyond this position, by arguing that the vagueness of general principles can be corrected by the study of actual case histories, claiming that *Manon Lescaut* is 'un traité de morale, réduit agréablement en exercice' (p.23). Yet in face of the pessimism which seems implicit in so much of Prévost's vision, the optimism of this argument looks rather forced, and the majority of critics who have commented on this highly contentious document are reluctant to take it as a full or even a sincere statement of Prévost's thought. Sermain has even claimed that Prévost is making a mockery of orthodox morality by supporting it with self-invalidating arguments (28). It is true that the *Avis* is merely one of many eighteenth-century novel prefaces which try to give a veneer of moral respectability to a genre held in low esteem and treating unedifying subject-matter. Such documents should always be taken with a pinch of salt. Yet there was a tradition in clerical circles whereby fiction could be used for edifying purposes, and Prévost was an admirer of Fénelon, its most illustrious representative. There are enough echoes of the *Avis* elsewhere in Prévost's work to suggest that he did reflect seriously along these lines, and in the 1753 edition of the work he appears to have tried to strengthen its aura of respectability by having it supplied with an allegorical frontispiece portraying Des Grieux caught between Manon and

Tiberge representing profane and sacred love respectively (*1*, pp.8–9). It is hard to believe that this adequately reflects the original inspiration of a work whose bleakly disabused vision of human nature is far removed from the bland conventionality of a moral tract, but it seems likely that the *Avis* expresses ideas which Prévost took seriously as a pious hope, as something he would like to be true even if he was not convinced that it was true. As a statement attributed to Renoncour rather than to Prévost himself, it makes better sense still. Renoncour in the final volumes has been fighting a losing battle to control the passions of Rosemont, a battle in which he has been reduced to uttering pious platitudes which he knows perfectly well are ineffective, and it would be in character for him to confront his unsettling experience of Des Grieux with consolingly high-sounding reflections which do not really come to grips with the problems raised.

In the end, the conflict between the three value-systems I have discussed in this chapter remains unsolved. Renoncour seeks to resolve it by a compromise which solves nothing, leaving Rosemont unhappy and himself cut off from the world in an inauthentic calm, whereas Des Grieux adopts the opposite strategy of opting for one of the codes and defying the others, leaving Manon dead and himself alienated from this world and perhaps the next as well. Each of the two narrators highlights the inadequacy of the other's strategy, and none of the value-systems under consideration seems able to offer its adherents a sustainable or a satisfactory life-style; they each have their good qualities, but of a kind which serves only to highlight the weaknesses of the other two codes. In these circumstances, Prévost stands little chance of being able to realize any edifying ambitions he may have had; he is simply not sure enough of the values he expresses. Instead, he has produced one of the rare genuinely tragic works of the eighteenth century, a two-fold tragedy of a couple who love each other in incompatible ways and whose love is incompatible with the values embodied by the world surrounding them. It expresses a vision of society whose values are in a state of flux, with an old hierarchical system in decline, having lost its moral authority, and no new system as yet in view to replace it, at least not in the eyes of the cautious and traditionally trained Prévost who is not quite yet a man of the Enlightenment. In terms of the message it expresses, the work is ambiguous and disappointing to the reader who will be satisfied with nothing less than total clarity. Yet in artistic terms it has proved itself an undeniable success, and in my final chapter I shall consider why this is so.

6. Why *Manon Lescaut?*

That *Manon Lescaut* survives as one of the most widely-read French novels while the rest of Prévost's fiction has, until recently, been out of print for a century and a half is one of the most intriguing anomalies of French literary history. Modern editions and a revival of critical attention have done much to rehabilitate his forgotten novels and allow a fairer judgment to be made, but there is as yet no serious attempt to deny the supremacy of *Manon Lescaut*, and the phenomenon needs to be explained.

One explanation that used to be popular, the theory that the work is autobiographical, must surely now be discounted. In *Manon Lescaut*, the theory runs, Prévost was telling his own story, thus achieving a spontaneity and an intensity of feeling not to be found in his other works which are governed more by fictional convention. Prévost's life story is still very incompletely known, and autobiographical allusions cannot be ruled out, but the close identity between life and work postulated by Harrisse has been shown to be methodologically unsound, and in the absence of any positive evidence in favour of it, it is best to seek other explanations. Admittedly the themes of *Manon Lescaut* seem to correspond to problems he faced in his own life, but these themes are present in all his works, and there is no reason to assume that *Manon Lescaut* is any more autobiographical than the others. Taken as a whole, his fiction shows considerable ability to incarnate these recurring themes in novel plots that are obviously invented, and it is likely that the same thing is happening in *Manon Lescaut*. Supporters of the autobiographical theory might perhaps point to the fact that *Manon Lescaut* comes at an early stage in Prévost's career as a novelist and suggest that this is a case, not infrequent in literary history, of an author who has put the essential of his experience of life into one successful first novel and then failed to renew himself in his subsequent works.

There may be an element of truth in this, but since a careful reading of Prévost's other novels reveals a growing rather than a declining technical sophistication as his career proceeds, it seems unlikely that this will do as a complete explanation.

Another possible source of superiority may lie in the work's supposed realism. It is set in a slightly less remote period than much of Prévost's fiction, about fifteen years before the time of writing and in an age and a place that Prévost himself knew. It thus is able to create a better impression of observed reality than Prévost's other, more convention-ridden novels, and in this respect it corresponds better to the subsequent expectations of the novel formed in the nineteenth century. This argument rings somewhat truer; *Manon Lescaut* does have less of the storms, shipwrecks, pirates and coincidental meetings which were the stock-in-trade of many novels of the period, including some of Prévost's own, and I have already suggested that the work achieves an effective representation of Des Grieux's Paris, even though description plays only a minor part in Prévost's concerns. Certainly the prominence he gives to money strikes an original note in the French novel; his serious treatment of that and other subjects traditionally felt to be fit only for burlesque fiction marks a considerable advance in what was possible within the novel. This, however, does no more than make him an interesting historical figure. It does not explain why *Manon Lescaut* is still read today by a readership familiar with novels which have realized far more ambitious mimetic effects, and it is simply not true that the date and place of the work are radically different from the rest of his output. None of his works go further than seventy years into the past — most seventeenth-century novels went much further back — and many of his works have the very blend of familiar and exotic settings that we find in *Manon Lescaut* itself. Some of his later novels attempt a far more systematic portrayal of Paris society in the recent past, and they are not his best works. In terms of realism, any difference between *Manon Lescaut* and the rest is one of degree, not of kind, and certainly not enough by itself to account for the work's unique success.

A more promising line of approach, emerging in the sixties with the work of Mylne, Sgard, Deloffre and Picard among others, dwells on the generic distinction between *Manon Lescaut* and Prévost's other fiction. I have referred to the work throughout this study as a novel, but the term is imprecise, and it needs to be recalled that *Manon Lescaut* is in fact an interpolated story in a longer novel and therefore governed by a different set of conventions. Prévost's longer novels can be seen as a last attempt to revive a declining tradition inherited from the seventeenth century, in which novels were long, often rambling in structure, based on cliché-ridden improbable stories and populated by characters who were excessively idealized owing to the genre's high-minded epic pretensions. *Manon Lescaut*, on the other hand, can be seen as a specimen of a shorter style of narration, often referred to as the *histoire*, in which the epic ambitions are less prominent and the approach less idealized, down to earth without being burlesque, and on occasions tragic. The *histoire* occurred frequently as an interpolated tale in a longer work, and the collection of seven *histoires* by Challe, entitled *Les Illustres Françaises*, has been rescued from undeserved critical oblivion and shown to be a major influence on both the theme and form of Prévost's masterpiece. The rediscovery of Challe has helped to free *Manon Lescaut* from the clutches of autobiographical interpretation, by showing that it is situated within a literary tradition rather than a work of total spontaneity. It has also situated Prévost's work within the evolving pattern of French realistic fiction by relating it to a group of stories which are often remarkable for their starkly matter-of-fact representation of ordinary life.

The present study is not the place for a full consideration of Prévost's sources or the merits of his other fiction; suffice it to say that the above argument is valid in its essentials, though it would be highly misleading to describe Prévost's longer novels solely in terms of the declining seventeenth-century tradition or to draw too sharp a distinction between the novel and the *histoire* as practised by Prévost; features of the two types of fiction mingle to some degree in most of his works. *Manon Lescaut* does, however, gain in two significant respects from its status as *histoire*, a word which does of course occur in its full title. First, considerations of scale and discipline are important, especially for a less leisured audience than the novel readers of the eighteenth century, who tolerated long-winded and unstructured fictional forms better, perhaps, than their descendants today. Prévost's other novels are not exceptionally long by the standards of their day, nor are they totally lacking in structure, but it is easy to see the advantage of a relatively short work whose story is in many respects more plausible and whose form is more readily graspable, based as it is on the conceptually simple device of repeated parallel episodes, which Prévost seems to have taken from the story of Des Frans and Sylvie in *Les Illustres Françaises*.

The other advantage of *histoire* over novel is that it frees Prévost from any kind of epic pretension. In his longer novels he seems to feel obliged to aim at a serious edifying tone and make his characters undergo a process of evolution whereby they solve some of the problems raised by their adventures. The picture I have drawn of *Manon Lescaut*, however, suggests that solving problems was not Prévost's strong point; Renoncour tries to claim that he has solved his, but it looks much more as if he has run away from them. The tragic resolution of Des Grieux's adventures, which does not need to impose some normative solution where none is readily available, may well lend itself better to effective aesthetic realization, and the *histoire* makes this kind of tragic dénouement possible. Prévost did not go on to write a series of tragic *histoires* in the vein of *Manon Lescaut*; for that he was too wedded to his ultimately futile quest for a more positive type of dénouement, for a clearer vision of human destiny which ultimately eluded him. It is significant, however, that the work of Prévost which most critics rate second best after *Manon Lescaut* is another *histoire* in a tragic vein, the *Histoire d'une Grecque moderne*.

Such an argument would offer one of the more convincing explanations of *Manon Lescaut*'s success. It seems to me, however, that the crucial factor is the brilliant marriage of form and content which Prévost has effected in this work. All of his major novels use the device of first-person narration, and in all of them Prévost takes considerable care to match the narrator's vision and style of narration with the story he has to tell and his character and situation as he tells it. With Des Grieux, however, the process is particularly successful. Des Grieux's narratorial situation is more clearly defined than most, set as it is within the *Mémoires d'un homme de qualité*, and given its closeness to events and the relationship he strikes up with the narratee, it is an unusually interesting one, to such an extent that the spectacle of Des Grieux telling his story is as much a part of the subject of the work as the story itself that he tells. The process of the narrator grappling with his past and trying to form a coherent image both of himself and his beloved is present in Prévost's other novels, but never more effectively dramatized.

As a result of this process, Prévost has been able to create two characters who have become archetypes. Manon stands at the beginning of a whole tradition of enigmatic *femmes fatales* and golden-hearted prostitutes who appear to love their men, often to a self-sacrificial extent, but never allow themselves to be completely possessed by them. It was a tradition which flourished especially in the nineteenth century in figures such as Carmen and Marguerite Gautier, both of whom, with Manon herself, have significantly been made into very successful opera heroines. The unknowability of Manon is the source of her charm; it reflects the sense of danger which appeals to men in certain types of women, and if it were possible to reduce Manon to a simple explanation, much of her appeal would be lost, at least to male readers. The sense of Manon's essential simplicity enhances the elusiveness and the appeal; Théophé in the *Histoire d'une Grecque moderne*, a similarly enigmatic heroine and in many ways more subtly realized, perhaps loses some of the impact of Manon because she is so much more obviously a complex character.

The Manon we perceive would, however, not exist without Des Grieux; she is less a picture of a woman than a picture of a picture, or more accurately the verbal construct which we have watched Des Grieux draw from her. Everything depends, in the end, on how effectively Des Grieux is realized, both as narrator and

protagonist, and here again Prévost's success in portraying the
agonized young man trying to make sense of an elusive reality but
perpetually foiled by his own limitations and bad faith has achieved
a considerable literary posterity, running well into the twentieth
century. Des Grieux is not the only or even the first unreliable first-
person narrator, but he does seem to inaugurate a variation of the
type particularly successful in French literature, in which the attention of a male narrator is centred on an elusive and fragile love-
object in a short, disciplined and tragic story raising serious moral
themes; the tradition runs from Constant's *Adolphe*, through
Carmen, to the *récits* of Gide. There is a strong family resemblance
between Des Grieux and most of Prévost's narrator-heroes; the same
passionate blindness and the same moral uncertainties constantly
recur. What appears to mark out Des Grieux is the peculiarly single-
minded intensity with which he sets out to play his role as a hero of
love; the others all make more effort to compromise with other
values, or are less forcefully motivated by the women in their lives.
One may not like Des Grieux for this; some readers may be shocked
at his unorthodoxy, annoyed by his incorrigible weakness and
recidivism, irritated by his rhetoric or simply unconvinced of the
quality of the love by which he claims to be possessed. Prévost
himself may well share some of these dislikes. Nevertheless the role
Des Grieux plays, that of a man who has sacrificed all for love,
exercises a dangerous fascination and embodies an option which
many men are tempted to live out at some stage of their lives, even
though for most of the time they are thoroughly relieved not to be
involved in all the hard choices that such a role implies. Des
Grieux's appeal lies in the way he lives through this deep-seated
temptation.

The pleasure to be obtained from reading *Manon Lescaut*
appears, then, to be threefold. First, there is the pleasure of resolv-
ing an enigma, of trying to make sense of a world and of a heroine
to which we are given only incomplete clues. Admittedly for the
kind of reader who demands clear-cut solutions to problems the
pleasure here will be correspondingly incomplete, but once the
reader can accept this situation — as many twentieth-century

readers have learned to do — there is still much pleasure to be gained from the ever-renewed attempt to grasp the essence of this early incarnation of the *ewig-weibliche* — the eternal feminine. Secondly, there is the pleasure of vicarious identification with Des Grieux's dangerous but fascinating attempt to live out the role of ideal lover in a way that few dare to do in their own lives; it is easier to sympathize with behaviour such as Des Grieux's in the pages of a novel than it would be if we encountered it among our real-life acquaintances, and it is a well-recognized function of works of art to provide a cathartic acting-out of these darker areas of human desires. Finally, the work offers the pleasure of watching the dramatic interplay of conflicting value-systems. Again, the interplay is not resolved in such a way as to satisfy those who aspire above all to intellectual neatness; but by its refusal to impose inauthentically over-simple moralizing solutions, the work captures some of the richness and ambiguity of life itself, and it offers a psychologically coherent exploration of a significant problem. Whether any moral benefit accrues to the reader from being induced to face this problem, as Prévost wishes us to think that he hoped it would, is an enigma beyond the scope of this study.

Select Bibliography

EDITIONS

The following are essential complements to the Garnier-Flammarion edition:

1. *Histoire du Chevalier des Grieux et de Manon Lescaut*, edited by F. Deloffre and R. Picard (Paris, Garnier, 1965). Substantial, authoritative introduction, notes and variants.
2. *Mémoires d'un homme de qualité*, edited by J. Sgard. In Prévost, *Œuvres*, Vol. I (Presses Universitaires de Grenoble, 1978). Allows *Manon Lescaut* to be read in its original context; contains variants.
3. Prévost, *Œuvres, Vol. VIII* (Presses Universitaires de Grenoble, 1986). Contains J. Sgard's notes to 2.

CRITICAL WORKS ON PRÉVOST

What follows is merely a highly selective fraction of an immense field. For full bibliographical details, see *13*, *35*, and *36*. None of the many good general works on eighteenth-century fiction have been included.

4. *L'Abbé Prévost: actes du colloque d'Aix-en-Provence, 20 et 21 décembre 1963* (Gap, Ophrys, 1965). Important and varied collection of articles.
5. C.J. Betts, 'The cyclical pattern of the narrative in *Manon Lescaut*', *French Studies*, 41, 1987, pp.395–407. Shows how patterns of repetition are used as devices contributing to plot and character.
6. P. Brady, *Structuralist Perspectives in Criticism of Fiction. Essays on 'Manon Lescaut' and 'La Vie de Marianne'* (Bern, P. Lang, 1978). Collection of articles, with interesting methodological reflections as well as criticism of the text.
7. H. Coulet, 'Le thème de la 'Madeleine repentie' chez R. Challes, Prévost et Diderot', *Saggi e ricerche di letteratura francese*, 14, 1975, pp.287–304. Argues the case for a genuinely penitent Manon.
8. P. Creignou, 'La mauvaise foi dans *Manon*', *Europe*, 549–50, 1975, pp.175–89. Harsh Sartrian analysis of the deficiencies of Des Grieux.

9. S. Delesalle, 'Lectures de Manon Lescaut', *Annales: économies, sociétés, civilisations*, 26, 1971, pp.723–40. Important study of Manon in the context of her society.

10. J.I. Donohoe jr, 'The death of Manon, a literary inquest', *L'Esprit créateur*, 12, 1972, pp.129–46. Suggestive exploration of Des Grieux's mixed motives in his attitude to Manon.

11. J. Ehrard, 'L'avenir de Des Grieux: le héros et le narrateur', *Travaux de linguistique et de littérature*, 13, 1975, pp.491–504. Perceptive attempt to distinguish between Des Grieux as hero and as narrator.

12. B. Fort, 'Manon's suppressed voice; the use of reported speech', *Romanic Review*, 76, 1985, pp.172–91. Shows how Des Grieux deprives Manon of a voice by refusing to allow her direct speech.

13. R.A. Francis, 'The Abbé Prévost, 1968–1986; the present state of studies', *Studies on Voltaire and the Eighteenth Century*, 260, 1989, pp.381–425. Bibliographical comment on the recent period.

14. ——, *The Abbé Prévost's First-Person Narrators. Studies on Voltaire and the Eighteenth Century*, 306, 1993. Des Grieux seen in the context of Prévost's other narrators.

15. S. Gasster, 'The practical side of Manon Lescaut', *Modern Language Studies*, 15, 1985, pp.102–09. Presents Manon as an effective businesswoman.

16. F. Germain, 'Quelques mensonges de Manon', in *Mélanges littéraires François Germain* (Éditions Universitaires de Dijon, 1979), pp.15–28. The case against Manon, ingeniously argued.

17. J.P. Gilroy, *The Romantic Manon and Des Grieux. Images of Prévost's heroine and hero in nineteenth-century French literature* (Sherbrooke, Quebec, Naaman, 1980). The most substantial study of the novel's reception.

18. L. Gossmann, 'Prévost's *Manon*: love in the New World', *Yale French Studies*, 40, 1968, pp.91–102. Suggestive study of the function of the American episodes.

19. ——, 'Male and female in two short novels by Prévost', *Modern Language Review*, 77, 1982, pp.29–37. The hero's pursuit of the heroine parallels the reader's pursuit of meaning; an influential study.

20. H. Harrisse, *L'Abbé Prévost, histoire de sa vie et de ses œuvres* (Paris, Calmann Lévy, 1896). Pioneering biography, with important documents, but severely dated and suspect in some important areas. Should be read alongside *30*.

21. J. L. Jaccard, *Manon Lescaut (le personnage-romancier)* (Paris, Nizet, 1975). Lively, debatable exploration of how Des Grieux's attitude to his mistress and his story evolves.

22. H. Josephs, '*Manon Lescaut*: a rhetoric of intellectual invasion',
     Romanic Review, 59, 1968, pp.185–97. Explores the dialectic aims of
     the *Avis*.

23. J.R. Monty, *Les Romans de l'abbé Prévost: procédés littéraires et
     pensée morale*, *Studies on Voltaire and the Eighteenth Century*, 78,
     1970. Sets *Manon Lescaut* firmly in the context of the *Mémoires d'un
     homme de qualité*; takes a sharp critical view of Des Grieux.

24. V. Mylne, *Prévost: Manon Lescaut* (London, Arnold, 1972). A
     succinct, sound and reliable general study.

25. F. Piva, *Sulla genesi di Manon Lescaut* (Milan, Vita e Pensiero,
     1977). Important study of the work's genesis and the context of the
     Mémoires d'un homme de qualité; unfortunately limited to readers of
     Italian.

26. J. Proust, 'Le corps de Manon', *Littérature*, 1, 1971, pp.5–21.
     Influential and provocative study of the lovers' relationship.

27. N. Segal, *The Unintended Reader. Feminism and Manon Lescaut*
     (Cambridge University Press, 1986). A controversial reassessment
     with polemic elements; some suggestive readings of the text.

28. J.-P. Sermain, 'L'*Eloge de Richardson* et l'*Avis* de Renoncour en tête
     de l'*Histoire du Chevalier des Grieux et de Manon Lescaut*', *Cahiers
     Prévost d'Exiles*, 1, 1984, pp.85–98. Rigorously argued demolition of
     the *Avis*.

29. ——, *Rhétorique et roman au dix-huitième siècle. L'exemple de
     Prévost et de Marivaux*, *Studies on Voltaire and the Eighteenth
     Century*, 233, 1985. Prévost's treatment of the theme of eloquence;
     highlights an important area.

30. J. Sgard, *Prévost romancier* (Paris, Corti, 1968; 2nd edition 1989).
     Seminal work in modern Prévost studies, combining biography with
     thorough critical assessment.

31. ——, *L'Abbé Prévost. Labyrinthes de la mémoire* (Paris, P.U.F.,
     1986). Less biography and more literary assessment than *30*, with
     some important advances and revised opinions.

32. A.J. Singerman, 'A 'fille de plaisir' and her 'greluchon': society and
     the perspective of Manon Lescaut', *L'Esprit créateur*, 12, 1972,
     pp.118–28. Suggestive attempt to espouse Manon's point of view.

33. ——, *L'Abbé Prévost, l'amour et la morale* (Geneva, Droz, 1987).
     Rigorously argued exploration of the influence of Augustinian
     theology on Prévost; also suggestive on literary techniques.

34. P. Stewart, *Rereadings: eight early French novels* (Birmingham,
     Alabama, Summa, 1984). Contains a wide-ranging and sensitive essay
     on *Manon Lescaut*, pp.129–63.

35. P.J. Tremewan, *Prévost: an analytic bibliography of criticism to 1981* (London, Grant & Cutler, 1984). An indispensable and authoritative bibliographical survey, with critical comment.

36. ———, 'La critique prévostienne: 1982–1986. Une bibliographie analytique', *Cahiers Prévost d'Exiles*, 5, 1988, pp.61–83. Updating of *35*.

CRITICAL GUIDES TO FRENCH TEXTS

edited by
Roger Little, Wolfgang van Emden, David Williams